Stable
Relation

To Fynn
with spirit
Anna Blake

Anna Blake

Stable Relation

A memoir of one woman's spirited
journey home, by way of the barn

Author photo by Sheri Kerley
Cover photo by Anna Blake
Cover design and formatting by JD Smith

Published by Prairie Moon Press

All enquiries to annamarieblake@gmail.com

First published 2015

ISBN: 978-0-9964912-0-4

For my Grandfather Horse
and all the horses who brought us girls home.

Contents

Part One:

Full Moon Over Broken Glass

Midlife Crisis on the Freeway

Cruising on the freeway at ten a.m. on a Friday morning had the tangy taste of playing hooky. I hoped someone I knew would see me. It felt like I was finally on the right road and making up time. The oldies station was on a roll; sometimes a radio magically speaks the infinite truth of the universe song by song. The music catapulted me toward a blissful enlightenment, as long as I didn't listen to the lyrics too closely. I was driving with the windows rolled down, car dancing with the steering wheel, and howling along like a hound dog on trash day. I knew every single word.

Baby, It's You. (Sing it high…Sha-la-la-la-lah!)

The I-25 freeway, south from Denver, traced the front range of the Rockies, all mountains on the right side, and scrub oak hills and prairie on the left. There was a great view from this height, bobbing along on the bench seat of a big white pick-up truck—a conservative vehicle, American-made, and I naturally named it after my recently deceased father. The mechanical Lloyd was so much easier to get along with. Without a harsh word, Lloyd towed a past-prime horse trailer, filled with tack and buckets and feed, and best of all, a leopard Appaloosa named Spirit. I was on my way to the state fairgrounds in Pueblo for a horse show and a dream as old as me. My father never approved of my love of horses, but now Lloyd took me to horse shows and patiently parked for hours, finally bringing us safely back home. So much about a relationship can be improved post-death.

You Don't Own Me. (A matching head and index finger shake while cruising at 65 mph.)

There was a fleeting, but troublesome thought concerning my future. I'd spent a few years carelessly killing brain cells in early adulthood, and I wondered how many of the ones remaining were taken up with less than crucial information, like the words to these old songs. I needed my wits for the important work of balancing my checkbook and finding my car keys. What if the world came undone and the only help I could offer was the words to *Duke of Earl?*

The cooler was on the front floor board, packed with road-trip food. I put a root beer in the plastic cup-holder hooked on the window and opened the vegetarian pork rinds—some people call them Cheetos. It had taken me a while to get to this enviable position behind the wheel.

Little Deuce Coupe. (Doing *The Pony* on the bench seat, just with my sit-bones.)

I'd been magnetized to horses from my first pony, sold away by my parents, to my last childhood horse, a sweet mare who needed a new home before I graduated from high school. I knew when I left that I wouldn't be back. Then there were a few lonely years after leaving home before I could support a horse on my own. The longing never let me rest. Some of us are born with a piece missing. Mine is a horse-shaped piece and I searched for it like a missing twin. Now I was a grown-up, and when my horse homecoming day finally arrived, there were squeals and moans, the same breathless elation as when I got my first pony. But this time the decisions were all mine and I could put my time and money where my heart had always been.

I was a dangerous woman because I had all the enthusiasm of a twelve-year-old girl, but more vocabulary, hormones, and my own bank account.

Love Me Tender. (Elvis croons as deep and soft as the nicker of a mare.)

Now I had the horse, but I was living in a city with no barn in my backyard, so I found a boarding stable and started a different kind of horse life. I commuted out every day but Spirit had staff and I didn't muck or fix fence. We rode and grazed. I bought tack, riding lessons, show gear, more lessons, better tack, and even more lessons. I was having the time of my life, riding my passion at a hand-gallop and learning everything I could. Spirit and I made great progress. And I could have renovated a hundred-year-old house with less money.

I traded my vintage Cadillac for a truck and the next year, I got my first horse trailer. There were even more opportunities now that I could take him off property. Riding a horse always had an elevated feeling of freedom but now we could venture away to trail rides and horse shows, returning home Sunday nights, dusty and tired. It was like another layer of freedom.

Save the Last Dance for Me. (A shoulder-shimmy sort of slow dance.)

So, of course, I sang loud enough to drown out traffic sounds and scatter antelope along the way. It was a standout moment in time; I worked hard and I deserved it. Traffic was picking up and there was less space. I watched my mirrors and maintained brake distance, but every time I slowed up to increase the distance to the car in front of me, another car pulled in between us, and I had to back off again. It created the feeling that I was almost traveling backwards on the freeway and it still didn't dampen my mood. I even loved traffic.

Why must I be a teenager in love? (A pinkie finger dance on the wheel.)

A car pulled up in the fast lane, a Corvette with a T-top. It was cliché red. The man driving it had a bald spot on the back of his head—his comb-over flapped in the wind. This guy was such a living stereotype; *midlife crisis* could've been his vanity plate. He looked my way, lifted his gas foot and smiled, with all the confidence in the world. His belly rested against the steering wheel and I could tell by his head bob, he was singing along to the same song as me! Why wasn't he embarrassed? Listening to oldies was a charmingly eclectic habit for me, I was a baby in the fifties. He was old enough to date when he first listened to this music. Was he actually flirting with me?

I couldn't pull my eyes away, he sang louder and then brought a hand up to his brow and gave me a salute the same instant he dropped his foot to the gas pedal and roared ahead like a jet. Did that silly car really need four mufflers? It was laughable. He couldn't possibly think he was having the same sort of Friday that I was. So arrogant—I almost felt sorry for him.

I pumped my brake, to allow more room for the car in front and decelerated to an uncomfortable awareness. Was he that much older than me really? I certainly had more hair, but then mine was gray. What if I was driving my midlife crisis too? Only mine had the WT designation: Work Truck, vinyl upholstery, no rug. It came with no fantasy, or even an intention of grace. I bought it used. My horse trailer was faded blue with a silver interior, spray-painted over the rust, and only a few years younger than me. I noticed my singing voice wasn't as strong now.

The only thing worse than a midlife crisis is a poorly financed midlife crisis, and okay, my belly might be an inch closer to the steering wheel, too. It was very humbling to think that the Corvette comb-over was my brother-in-denial.

Bye Bye Love. (How did I not know this was such a sad song? They sound so chipper.)

How naïvely cynical I was that day, car dancing along. I might as well have been on black ice, where just skirting a pot-hole was enough to begin a slow motion spin, out of control, but with hang time enough to see the crash coming. Hindsight is bittersweet. My beautiful midlife crisis began quietly and by the time I recognized it, it was as undeniable as gravity. I couldn't tell if it was killing me or making me stronger.

My Best Days Might Not Be Ahead Of Me

But wait, I got ahead of myself. By way of introduction, I was the very last person anyone expected to have a midlife crisis. I had a perfectly enviable life. My dogs even came to work with me. I had good friends, a fairly successful art career, and the future looked bright. I'd always thought that the term midlife crisis was a punch line for a joke, something to do with the early bird special or an excuse for men behaving badly. I should have shown more respect.

An early bloomer, when my midlife crisis started I was thirty-nine years old. It came in the mail. During the second or third time my father had disowned me, depending on how you count, a letter arrived one ordinary day to inform me that my father was dying. Most families use telephones. Since it was during a time of estrangement, a letter must have felt safer to my mother, like she was disobeying my father a little less. The note said cancer. It was a reflex; I picked up the phone and called. Dad picked up the receiver on his end, heard my voice and slammed it down. It's hard to explain but it's true; I was his favorite.

The next afternoon I arrived at their trailer park in Arizona. My mother looked tiny and exhausted but we didn't hug. She started to tell me about my dad when she was interrupted by a loud thud in their bedroom. I followed her in to find that my dad had fallen from the bed. He was a shadow on the rug, just skin and bones with dark eyes and parched skin. I bent down and carefully lifted him back to the bed. I could tell he was embarrassed by his weakness. He lashed out, snarling that I was the last person he expected to see. I didn't take the bait. My voice stayed low, "The way you treated me, I'm not surprised."

Over the next few weeks, I cooked for him. I cut his hair. One of us said everything she needed to say, and one of us grew weaker. It worked like a truce. He never verbalized his love, but his caustic edges got softer before he faded away. Even cancer has an upside.

The largest part of my father's legacy came to me gradually. I inherited his depression. It gave me a quiet place to watch my life unravel in slow motion. In the next few years, I practiced loss as if it made me holy.

Later that year, as a dear friend lost her battle with cancer, I helped her tie up the loose ends of her life, as mine was coming apart. The economy faltered and my business and income followed suit. I had already purchased a second horse, Dodger, when our boarding barn sold, and my trainer and barn friends went to a more expensive facility. My two horses and I found a smaller, lonelier barn. After that my mother's cancer returned and there were more trips to the Arizona trailer park, more hopeless watching. She passed in the same month as my divorce was finalized.

I liked to think I was a multi-tasking, survivor sort of woman, ready to handle whatever life threw at me. I liked to think I could cope with stress better than most people. In the end, it didn't matter what I liked to think.

So much loss. When my very sweet, elderly dog was euthanized, it was harder than losing my mother or husband in some ways. For eighteen years, he was my shadow and he was a leaner. Without his shoulder pressed against my leg, I could barely find my balance. The landscape was unrecognizable for everything missing. I wasn't sure my best days were ahead of me.

Wearing the thinnest veneer of feigned confidence, I packed what was left of my life in a few boxes and moved into a tiny four-room house in a vintage neighborhood. It felt roomy. The yard had a huge old tree where I scattered my good dog's ashes and I started putting in a massive sandstone patio, rebuilding the ground. I couldn't shake the feeling of sliding on black ice. I needed the earth to give my feet some traction. The heavy manual labor solidified my pain into a manageable form and exhaustion finally gave me sleep. Then the final blow: I lost the lease on my studio and gallery. My landlord sold the building and the new owners wanted my storefront. It took a moment to sink in. After sixteen years there, I had no place to work.

To say I cried would have been an understatement, I was hysterical. It was that gasping, snot-choked, barking kind of bawl—satisfying and humiliating all at the same time. My skin turned red, my eyes swelled shut, and I fell into a heaving pile of despair. What I notice about crying is that there is a finite amount of adrenaline and eventually the tears subside. It took about an hour.

Almost audible, a tiny voice mumbled, "What if this isn't bad?" It might have been me but it was hard to tell in my dehydrated, yet soggy state. Besides I was carrying a few hundred extra pounds of depression around with me. It was a crazy notion. Again, a bit stronger, "What if this isn't bad?" I managed a shrug. I didn't have much holding me here. If there was someplace I would rather be, I didn't have much to pack. I took stock of my resources: no family, no husband, no workplace. What did I have to lose? I was forty-five years old with two horses and two dogs. My older horse's age would catch up with us one of these years, and living in a boarding barn wasn't his idea of a great retirement plan. What if I could find him a safe pasture of his own? The world was crumbling around me but if there was a home barn, a solid piece of earth for my little herd, we could get through this. Some place where the dogs could bark and the horses could run and I could regain my full height.

A home barn was a great idea! I was already paying a mortgage and board for both horses, which added up to the equivalent of two mortgage payments. In a rare moment of common sense, it seemed like a great financial decision and an unusual opportunity for a horse owner. There's nothing practical about keeping horses and the money side of the equation was just ridiculous. While patting myself on the back for putting horses and practicality together in the same thought, it never crossed my mind what moving to the country would do for my urban income.

I Could Make This Work

The next morning, I woke up early and cheerful. After breakfast, I wiped down my baseboards, cleaned the bathroom and made some phone calls. My house had a for-sale sign on it the next day and I was as good as gone.

The hunt for a farm felt very familiar. I'd been doing it since my family lost our farm on Leaf River in Minnesota. I was ten years old and it made no sense to me. It happened fast and I had to leave my pets behind. Our family settled on the edge of a town in Washington state, but I always kept a corner of our farm in my memory and looked for a match where-ever I went.

After I moved to Denver, I couldn't imagine a way I could live out of town but for the next twenty years, every time I drove past the city limits, I looked just the same. I drove right past farms with fresh paint and tidy yards that I knew were not meant for me. Every time I saw an empty, run-down farm house from the road, my car involuntarily slowed. A few of the windows might be boarded up and there was trash blown around. There was usually a dilapidated barn out back or maybe the skeleton of an old hen house. It was a failed farm; as familiar as home. It was the dream of living an authentic life. I surveyed the condemned property with a critical tilt to my head, and judged the work needed to make the place live-able. The farm was always worse than condemned, but each time my verdict was the same, "I could make this work." I'd do what it took to live in the country. It was a quiet affirmation that it wasn't too late. I'd do with less to go back to that old life and be the adult this time. Entire years went by when I didn't drive out of town at all, and avoided the lust for a failed farm all together. It was a desire too dear to name, too precious to ask for. Until now, forty-five years old and nothing left to lose.

Hours evaporated in front of my computer as I studied the market. Where were the farms for arty girls with a limited budget and big plans? This property had to work on my income without cutting my riding budget too much. In the Denver area, that meant the properties that were at least an hour away out on the flat, windy, treeless prairie. Some properties had old farm houses but most of them had a double-wide trailer—a modular home, if you want to be politically correct.

After calling on the first few properties, I noticed real estate agents weren't any more interested in me than the popular jocks in high school had been. Apparently the commission on a property in my price range did not rate the gas expense. They gave me directions to gravel roads on the edge of nowhere, and I loaded my two cattle dogs, Spam and Hero, in the truck and we showed ourselves around. The land to the northeast was good, but many of the small acreages were corners. Corners are what are left when farmers plant in those crop circles you see from airplanes. That part appealed to me, I could see crop circle art in my future. The properties were about five acres, but the triangular shape made them seem half that big. The best ones had an old farm house in the biggest area. There were usually trees, but there was no room for a riding arena.

My other option was to buy empty land, and assemble my own pre-fab farm. That route didn't meet the immediate gratification requirement.

Most properties that I saw online were sold when I called and the conversations were brief. I called on a property to the southeast early one morning and the realtor who picked up the phone told me that that particular property was sold, but she sounded kind of excited about it. Then she said she'd be *really happy* to get some properties together to show me. She was enthusiastic, she was focused. She was probably very new on the job.

I met her later that week and immediately felt under-dressed. The realtor had perfect hair, a dress-for-success suit, and pumps. She looked great, but it was possible that rural property was not her usual neighborhood. As good as her word, she showed me a list of seven properties, all in my price range, all horse legal. She offered to drive, until she saw Spam and Hero panting and smiling in my truck. She quickly weighed the options and came along with me. Less dog hair in her new car that way; it would all be on her suit instead.

The first property on the list was stick built, a term used for a house not delivered on wheels. This house had two different kinds of siding and the paint on them almost matched. The owner opened the front door and welcomed us in. I stepped through the door, and as the realtor crossed the threshold behind me, it happened. It was a quiet gagging sound as... *Her breath caught in her throat.* I always wondered what that phrase meant when I read it in novels.

She saw the same room I did, but it just surprised her more. The living room contained an unmade twin bed, a weight-lifting machine with men's tighty-whities drying on it, and a life-sized poster of a naked woman on a Harley. There was a good chance that the owner was single. We began our tour. The bedroom had extra-extra plush carpet, the top layer of multi-green shag with a layer of multi-orange shag underneath. It wasn't nailed down so changing the décor wouldn't be a problem. Besides the master bedroom, there were two half-bedrooms. The kitchen stove was relatively clean, except for some hot sauce splatters, and there was fresh peel-and-stick linoleum on the floor.

We went out the back door and past a line of chain-link dog runs. There was a beautiful pond with trees around the south side, just on the far side of a sharp ravine, deep enough to bury a few cars. To the right, there were several cargo shipping containers lashed together to make a shed, surrounded by piles of old lumber and rolls of used wire. A water hydrant was positioned close by the yard light. No animals lived here now, but the strategically placed bath-tubs remained. The owner had built a large three-sided shed with four bays for his trucks, each one about the size of a horse stall. It didn't take a lot of squinting to see it as a barn. I went to the highest, flattest part of the property and marched off the length and width of a dressage arena. It fit with a few feet to spare.

When we got back in the truck, the realtor apologized immediately, "I had no idea the place was such a disaster," she said. "He must live there alone. I did think the kitchen had potential." Maybe she thought that would appeal to me, but I told her I didn't like to cook. And other than the trash, this place had a lot that worked for me. Her relief and confusion were almost balanced.

We spent the day looking at old houses, double-wides, and sheds that were almost barns. On one of the stops, I was marching off the property in a grassy area, counting steps for an arena, and up ahead Hero fell in a hole. He jumped out and trotted on, but in a few steps, I fell in the same hole. It was an old post hole big enough to fit a foot, and knee deep. I lumbered back to my feet and continued counting. A minute later I heard a little shriek, and the realtor fell in that same hole, in her sweet little pumps. I took it as a sign that we were all on the same path and this realtor was tougher than she looked. We were fading a bit by one o'clock, so we stopped at a gas station, got a pair of hot dogs and kept going. I marched off distances, checked well depths, and made notes. Most of all, I tried to visualize my horses there.

A look inside of other people's homes can be warm and welcoming, or it can be painfully personal. After a full day of the latter, our hearts hurt as much as our feet. The homes ranged from new modulars that felt like motel rooms to well-used homes with worn furniture, stained carpet, and old paint. Sometimes the smell said it all. There's a fine line between opportunity and desperation sometimes.

The properties split into two groups: Fairly marginal homes with a fairly marginal barn or slightly better houses with no barn at all. As we drove back to the office in town, my realtor and I rehashed the properties. She was sure she could find more in my price range, still optimistic. I was more pragmatic. This was what was available for my money and I thought one would work.

I picked my favorite in each group and went for a second look alone two days later. The first possible was a brand new, foreclosed modular home with fresh vinyl wallpaper and a full frame view of Pikes Peak. No one was living there, so I walked the land again and visualized a barn, a full size arena, and the cost to build them. On the plus side, I'd never lived in a place this new.

Then over to the other possibility, the first place the realtor showed me. I parked on the dirt road out front, looking across the would-be arena and the south pasture. I remembered the Harley poster. This place would become a collector's home; it's rare to find a one bathroom house these days. From this angle, the pond was hidden by a pile of broken pallets. Still, waterfront property is pretty uncommon on the Colorado prairie and it did have that homey, failed farm look about it. *I could make this work.*

Full Moon Over Broken Glass

It was a ninety-minute drive back to my house in Denver and I didn't car dance once. First I called the realtor and made my offer. The decision felt right; there was peace with a delicate fringe of hysteria. Then I dug out the ad I'd been saving for used fence panels. Each panel was twelve feet long, five feet tall, and made of a heavy gauge steel. Joined together, it's a sturdy, safe pen for the horses. I did quick math with the dimensions of the truck shed, and gave the man a call. He agreed to deliver the panels in a month and I dropped off a check for $1000.00 on the way home. I meant it as an affirmation, a kind of *build it and they will come* push to set my change in motion. It seemed totally logical that if I had a pen, the farm deal would follow.

My realtor called the next evening. The owner accepted my first offer, but was in no hurry to sell. What did that mean? Maybe his reluctance was obvious in hindsight; the property wasn't exactly staged for a quick sale. I had a medium-large size rant brewing and my voice was already an octave higher.

"Why list it then!?"

My realtor, strong enough to eat gas station hot dogs, confirmed that she had a mission she intended to complete and my voice returned to its normal range.

She asked what stipulations I wanted in the contract. What? My previous home purchases had no stipulations, but then, this property had a hoarder quality with large piles of scrap wood and wire. In my *I could make this work* brain, I assumed what I saw was what I got. My realtor's expectations were much higher and the list only started with hauling off the trash. I imagined her smile as she asked, "*Professional* house cleaning?"

I hadn't felt like there'd been anyone on my side for a while, but I did now. She didn't get adversarial with the owner, instead she just relentlessly nudged him along and politely thanked him for each step—I train horses the exact same way. Paperwork was signed, inspections were scheduled, and the closing date was set for high noon on Halloween. I joyously looked forward to paying her commission.

My house hadn't sold yet so I raided my savings for the down payment on the farm and found renters for my Denver house.

The morning of escrow closing, I packed the truck with enough tools, paint, cleaning supplies, and camping gear to make a start inside the house. Would there be trick-or-treaters? Just in case, I bought some Halloween candy. I had a kitten in a cat carrier. Spirit had befriended him at the old boarding barn, sharing his grain with him for the last couple of weeks. He was a tiny stray who volunteered to come along and be in charge of varmint control.

At the last minute a friend dropped off a housewarming gift: A bottle of champagne with two cured pig ears tied to it, so Spam, Hero, and I could all celebrate. One last look at the boxes stacked for the movers, and I closed the door soundly behind us. The dogs were ecstatic; they knew a road trip when they saw one. I tuned the radio to a country station this time, and cranked it up.

The papers were signed and dated, again and again, and I agreed to pay a large sum with interest. It felt less like a debt, and more like a license to change. I gave my realtor a ball cap as a thank you present—I think it might be the first one she'd ever owned. It had the words "Boss Mare" on it. I explained what it meant; that horse herds were run by the alpha mare, recognizable because she is the one who moves everyone else's feet. I know my boss mare went through at least one pair of pumps doing it. She hugged me, I hugged her, thanks all around, big smiles, and a fist pump as I climbed back into my truck to go home.

The view was somewhat different on this side of the paperwork. I carried a load from the truck into the house and looked around. The best I can say is that the previous owner had moved out. The bathroom was *un*professionally cleaned, along with about half of the kitchen. Not the fridge half, so my food stayed in my cooler. I stood in the doorway and stared at the oil stains on the living room floor.

Was this the first time I had stood still in the last month? I heard the dog's toenails clicking in and out of the rooms with a scurried rhythm, rushing from one interesting smell to another. Not all of the agreements in the contract were met, but it was too late to complain about it now.

I walked the property with the dogs, stopping to ponder the crazy month that landed us here and to pick up litter as we went. The sky was massive and the land was flat and open, with nothing hidden in any direction. The farm felt simple and uncomplicated. Each time my arms filled with trash, I took a lap past the garage and added to the pile there. We walked to the ravine, and the dogs plowed down the bank and ran into the pond. A ravine this deep could easily break an unsuspecting horse's leg, but it could be filled and leveled.

The sky was an immense cavern of pure air and the more I breathed it in, the more my chest expanded. Muscles let loose and my ribs got flexible. How long had my shoulders been up next to my ears? I felt a little cleaner with each exhale.

I looked back toward the house. Was that a car in the driveway? Did I have company already? Maybe a friend came to congratulate me! I hurried to the driveway out front and found the seller's agent with a key. They forgot to give it to me at the closing. He explained that it was the front door key, and no, the back door didn't have a lock. Before I could ask what the point of locking the front door would be, he was gone.

That's when the prairie got very quiet. I started a book of

lists, my form of passive hysteria. I started with a list of the lists I needed to make: things to do before the movers came, things to do before the horses came, things I needed from the hardware store, things I needed to do before I felt normal.

By the time I finished, it was almost dusk and the air was cooling. We went to the front porch steps to wait for trick-or-treaters. It was silly; I had only been there two hours, not long enough to know there were no neighbor kids. Spam and Hero had their dinner while I pawed through the cooler. I grabbed some cheese and bread along with our dessert of pig ears and champagne. The dogs did their best wiggle-sit for their treats, and I popped the cork and poured my treat into a coffee mug. Then, with almost no fanfare at all, a full moon rose at the end of my driveway. It was impossibly huge, glowing with a rich apricot color. It took gloriously long, heavy moments to clear the horizon, until it snapped away and floated up, lighting the pasture like the sun. An owl flew to the tree by the driveway. That line came again... *Her breath caught in her throat,* only this time it was me. The sky got even bigger as stars came out, and coyotes sang by the pond. We cast a moon shadow, the dogs and I together, and the earth softened to hold us safe. My eyes dropped down to the flower bed at the edge of the front deck. It was scattered with a dozen broken beer bottles, glittering in the moonlight.

In Praise of Virgin White

The clock was ticking. Only thirty-six hours until my appointment with the movers back in Denver. I went to work on the inside of the house but at times it felt more like an exorcism than cleaning. The walls were sticky with dirt and smoke. I wanted a flame thrower, or at least a pressure washer. I scrubbed the entire house and when that was done, I changed the water and scrubbed again. I carried a razor-blade scraper for the thick spots. The walls were finished with a bleach water rinse and when that was drying, I made an emergency run for shelf paper so I could rest a bit while driving. Sure, the previous owner had a casual approach to housekeeping, but my zealousness had very little to do with the history of this house, and much more to do with the mess of my life. I was cleaning with a vengeance. Dogs marked their territory and I marked mine. I needed a clean start.

It had been really easy to pick paint colors. Some people look at a store display of paint chips for hours, and ponder the difference between Winter White and Antique White. Or get a sample size and bring it home to paint on and look at it for a while. Would Ecru do or was Eggshell more passive? There are warm whites and cool whites, and an entire collection of off-white colors with names meant to evoke beauty and peace, but they might as well all be called Loss of Innocence White. There was no question in my mind, for this job there was one choice: just plain white—the color things are in the beginning.

No contrasting walls. Design and finesse could happen later. For now it was about retaliation over plaster cracks, over years of fingerprints on doorways, over life before now. It was like painting over a dark color, only Virgin White could do the job, in two coats, maybe three.

First, I did prep work repairing the cracks in every room and taping windows and edges. The tarp went down on the floors, and I donned the sacred paint outfit; my best worn out jeans, a favorite stained T-shirt and a rakish bandanna to cover my hair. I surveyed my brushes, rollers, stuffed a few rags in my pockets and shook out my shoulders and arms like a boxer before the bell rings. Finally, I opened the first five gallon bucket and poured thick, pristine white paint into my pan. I paint walls like other people run marathons.

I started at the front end of the house. I painted the "master" bedroom, where two walls were cracked original plaster and two were new textured drywall. At least the color matched now.

There was a synthetic black-and-white wood paneling in the dining room. Maybe you could call it retro, but that would be false flattery—it was a fad that never caught on. It looked more like a zebra than natural wood, and it diminished a lovely window view of the south pasture and gave the room the feel of eating in a dirt cellar. Three coats required in this room.

Growing up, my mother was always re-painting rooms, altering colors, and then rearranging furniture. You would be gone for part of a day and come home to a different living room—but it never changed us. Sunny yellows and minty greens clashed with our family badly, but it was what she could do. I learned my love of white paint from my gallery. It cleans the air and adds size to the square footage, and is the perfect background for art. That was the plan for this house: make a piece of found-object art out of the parts of my life that had survived the move.

I was running on caffeine and Halloween candy, and making good time. The bathroom was quick; I had already bleached out the mold above the shower. Toward the back of the house, the seller had thrown in couple of walls to create the illusion of other bedrooms, just enough to count in the real estate listing. There were two of them—half-bedrooms—on either side of the bathroom. Each had almost enough room for one twin bed and one dresser. One had a half-closet, ceiling to waist and the other had a real, full-length closet, but the water heater was already in it. The walls had a texture sprayed on them, with a memory of paint mixed in. Now sealed in a white semi-gloss, the walls felt more substantial—maybe even permanent.

When I got to the back door, I peeled off my paint clothes and hit the shower for the first time at this house. I was a tub-soak sort of girl, and proud of it. Personal bathing habits are a huge quality of life question and showers never seemed like enough water to me. But I hung a new shower curtain and stepped in. The water was hot and the pressure just right. I stood there letting the water soften the paint on my arms and hair, gazing out the window. Yes, there was a window in the shower and it had a great view of the truck shed that would be my barn.

The only improvement this shower needed was an immediate view of my horses out that window. It was well past midnight and the hot water held up as long as I did. My bath towel pulled me together until I got into my camp cot but then my exhausted extremities let loose of each other and the thoughts in my head gave up trying to make sense. I can't say that I slept well, but I was content and numb and that passed for peace.

In the morning, the new paint smell was as welcoming as bacon. I drove back to my old house to watch the movers load my worldly possessions. Four and a half short hours later, my boxes, art, rugs, and clothes were stacked in their appropriate rooms at the farm and the movers were gone.

Movers are gods—I had no idea. My usual move involved me and anyone I could bribe to help, hauling load after load, until I was exhausted before the unpacking even started. This move, I didn't feel strong enough to ask for help and the drive was farther than across town. It's exactly how a splurge became a necessity. And these movers actually had the ability to alter reality for someone who seriously did everything the hardest way possible. By sunset, my art was hung and my home was habitable.

The Last, Best Load

It was like walking down the street with one foot on the curb and one in the road. I lurched with a jerky limp between settling into my farm and shutting down the last bits of my old life in Denver.

Every fall at the gallery I created a new collection of one-of-a-kind gold rings, earrings, and pendants for the holiday season. Goldsmithing was perfect work for me. It was self-motivated and creative, with the freedom to be noisy and dirty while soldering, forging, and polishing. Days were hectic as I finished all the holiday work, told everyone the story of my move to the farm, and the location of my one-day-a-week studio after Christmas. It was traditionally a busy time but this season it was particularly important to finish on a high note. I had to vacate my storefront at the end of the year, but there were still the busiest two months to get through first. It meant leaving the farm before dawn and coming home after dark, working extreme hours and then driving the three hour commute on top of that. I saw the horses at their barn when I could, and worked on my home barn in any leftover time available. I struggled to find balance on the uneven, in-between place. So far, this move was not a dream come true.

Every third or fourth day, utter exhaustion got the best of me. I stumbled into my dark house, collapsed onto the sofa, and the tears would start. I had never been the weepy sort, but I'd become a gusher at night. And this is after crying randomly and without warning through the day.

Most of the tears in my life had been spent in anger and the depth of my sadness now was disarming me, so I was whiny about that as well. It didn't feel like there was a bottom to the hurt and there was no reasoning with these tears; I could find no balance. I didn't live in Denver anymore, but I didn't actually live on the farm either. Somehow this move to live with the horses meant that I never got to see them. What had I done? All this crying made me mad, not that adding even more emotion did me any good.

No matter how much work I finished, not enough got done, and then I made lists about that. Tears and exhaustion gave way to sleep eventually, and my bed was only ten steps away, but I just couldn't get past the sofa. A few hours later, some limited amount of consciousness returned, along with a sore neck and swollen eyes. Then it was time to drive again, with a good chance I'd cry in the car.

I was holding my breath until my horses could come so I kept my head down and pushed on. I attacked the truck shed next. The stack of good luck fence panels that had been laying on the ground for a month were finally standing as a pen, supported by wooden posts buried in cement. The gate was open and waiting. The barn faced south so the sun warmed it early, and it blocked the north wind. There was fresh air and warmth, not like the closed up stalls the horses were used to. They could stretch out and nap in the sun here.

I'd have the ravine filled in soon, so the ground would be safe. The perimeter fence was still dangerous barb wire, but I set a few posts and steadied the wire. It was strong enough for now. Then I installed a gate at the end of the driveway, a literal line between us and the world. There was no money for any sort of cross fencing, but I didn't want the farm cut into a line of smaller fenced pastures. I wanted us all to live together in a huge pasture. I wanted them to be able to come up on the deck and look in my windows.

Everything wasn't perfect, but it was time for the horses to come, for one simple reason: I couldn't stand being without them any longer. Once they were here, it would all make sense, it would be easier. I put the finishing touches on their pen; fresh water from our well and rich alfalfa hay in the feeders. Then I hooked up the trailer for the last and best load.

The horses had been staying at a friend's barn, half-way between Denver and my new farm. Her offer to keep them there was more than a favor; it meant that I could see them briefly on my commute. I could at least do a drive-by nose scratch on the way home sometimes.

I pulled up her driveway, and started thanking her before I got out of the truck. We understood, each of us. Her horse property had been a while coming as well, and lending us a half-way place was a way she could do me a good turn, and be grateful for her barn at the same time. I hoped she heard my thanks at the blaring volume intended.

We loaded up and drove less than an hour to our new farm. Any farther and I would have needed a relief driver. I was too excited to sit still. Every inch of my skin vibrated with anticipation. My eyes darted to the rear view mirror and through the small window into the front of the trailer, but I couldn't see enough of them to read their body language. I listened, I hoped. What would the farm look like to them? They would love the pasture, wouldn't they? And I wanted them to think the barn was roomy and open. I'm not the sort to anthropomorphize too much. I don't dress my animals up in little sailor suits and make them eat at the table, but this was big. I'd never gotten an animal such an epic present before.

I was feeling fairly positive, even in my teary mess. Obviously they wouldn't care about the state of the house or its electrical problems. The fact that the garage was built over the top of the septic wouldn't concern them. I knew this barn wasn't as fancy as their boarding barn had been but the pasture was all theirs. I hoped that they would see me through the windows of the house and feel safe.

We pulled in and parked by our new home barn. I went to the back of the trailer and opened Spirit's door. He backed out quietly and I caught his lead rope as I opened Dodger's door and he stepped back. Both horses looked from one prairie horizon, to the long, flat, other prairie horizon, passively curious about my emotional state. I looked at them expectantly, hardly able to contain myself.

The area seemed normal enough, but why was the human so rattled? I led them to the lucky pen and took off their halters. Nope, they could tell it wasn't a show, no other horses, no other trailers or humans. And yet their human was pretty upset. Still, being confused was no reason to ignore the fresh water and green hay.

Okay, it was just me that was excited. The rest of us had no idea where we were. I basked in their smell and the touch of their shoulders. I got horse hair on my clothes, and smiled at their healthy manure. All of the stress and goodbyes and the doubt about how I would make a living here were dwarfed by the tactile reality of a curry comb scrubbing the neck of *my* horses, in *my* barn, on *my* farm. That night I walked to the window overlooking the pen again and again, checking on them, awestruck at this miracle of horses out the window. Without a thought, I walked past the quilt on the sofa and all the way to my bed for the first time at the farm, and I slept deep and soft.

The next day, the horses looked around waiting for something to happen, but nothing did. There was no show, no barn help, no other human nose-scratchers or treat-givers. Worst of all, there was no sign of their usual horse friends. The boys got a bit restless, Spirit looking from one direction to the other, checking the horizon for signs of life. Dodger, the younger horse, ate less and began to pace the fence line.

The stupefying quiet of small farm life was a let down after busy barn society. It wasn't their dream to be away from the herd—they were starting to fray. A sense of loss began to settle in. Horses don't like change any more than humans do. There was no way I could explain my plan to them, that living here would be peaceful and clean. I should have known. It doesn't matter if the change is good or bad, and the future is not the point. Horses know that right now is the only moment that matters. They're Buddhist that way.

A day later, Spirit started to be more comfortable. He was initially nervous but I told him, "This is all for you!" enough times that he got bored. He had a previous tendon injury and was a bit sore and uneven when he moved, so I watched him closely, hand walked him a couple of times a day, and let him graze some.

I did the same with Dodger, but with worse results. He was a confident, social horse, even a bit of a show-off. It's a wonderful quality for a competitor. But here, he might as well have been totally alone. He was devastated, and Spirit and I were no help at all. His initial pacing became more frantic and compulsive. His hooves showed the wear and damage within a few hours, but he didn't stop. For the first time in his life, he was nervous. He called and called for his herd, and with each whinny, I felt more guilt. My plan was a disaster. He only wanted his herd back.

As Dodger got more nervous, Spirit began to think Dodger knew something he didn't, so he paced along, sharing Dodger's anxiety. There were short breaks to eat and I tried to make sure they were drinking enough, but the ruts along the edge of the pen told me all I needed to know.

I started riding them, hoping that the old routine of work would settle them down but I had no arena and the hard ground was not a help. Horses have small and rather fragile feet, even with shoes on, work on hard or uneven ground puts stress on their hooves and legs. It was like they were on a hundred-mile ride inside their own paddock and riding them outside of it was a marginal help.

Each day since the move had been filled with bravado and depression, with hope and horror. I craved some middle ground; being jerked between extremes left me battered, and even more damp around the eyes. It wasn't just that all my problems had moved here with me, now I had created a few new ones.

My previous vet had given me a referral number for a local veterinarian. I had hoped to meet him with a simple vaccination, meet-and-greet sort of farm call, not a quirky and nebulous lameness check—but there was no choice. The new vet came a couple days later, but he didn't have the radiograph equipment with him. Reschedule. A second visit and he remembered the equipment, but he was uncertain about doing it at my farm. Finally he confessed that I should haul Dodger to his clinic.

Vets don't always have the best people skills so I gave him the benefit of the doubt. A couple days later, we hauled over to his clinic. The examination began in a paved area where the vet tech moved Dodger away and back, walking and trotting. It was easy to hear the uneven rhythm of his hooves on the pavement. Standing beside the vet, and past impatient, I said, "It's his right front, down low, maybe his hoof or fetlock, but his shoulder looks sore, too."

The vet stopped looking at my horse and faced me, "You can see that?"

We eyeballed each other, assessing what the other knew. Dodger seemed a bit dubious of the vet as well. I was a knowledgeable rider by then, with a good working understanding of equine bio-mechanics under my belt. The kind of horse owner who boards at barns with good reputations and competes strong and happy horses. Maybe he was used to a different kind of horse owner on trashy little farms like mine but my horses deserved better than a vet who was used to treating hogs.

We hauled home and rolled to a stop in front of the barn. I surveyed all that was mine: chain-link dog kennels, wooden shipping containers with metal straps cinching in bowed plywood, strewn car tires, parts of old doors, and tarps half buried in the dirt. The wind cleaned away the odors and worked like static to dull my ears. I felt hollow.

I'd dragged my boys to this disaster of a farm, and now both of them were lame and depressed to show for it. Years of careful training and the best care, and this was how far we had fallen in a few days. My dogs plopped down on my feet, and for the umpteenth time, I cried at my huge mistake. I was failing all of us. Still more tears. This silly crying was out of control. It had become my default response; any place, any time, big goober tears started with no warning. Enough with the crying already! I was sick and tired of mourning everything. This would have been a great time to quit and go back, but I had nothing to go back to.

I wiped my nose on my sleeve and stood up. When you get bucked off you climb back on; it was what I knew. I gave the horses some hay and went back to work. I took my hurt and my fear, and used it to rip out one of those dog runs. It was a fair sized task. The chain link was buried under the ground, with cinder blocks holding it down. I shoveled, and pulled until the wire left marks on my gloves, and then dug some more. Finally I tied the chain link to my truck bumper and pulled. Whoever these runs were built for, it was a prison.

Home for Christmas

The closer I got to the end of that year, the more bi-polar my world became. I dreaded, yet looked forward to the holiday. I was sad, yet elated that Christmas Eve was my last day at the gallery. I'd miss city life yet I couldn't wait to get away. I was glad it was my last daily three hour commute, yet I was sure I'd miss the drive. I got to be at the farm full time, and yet I *had* to be at the farm full time. The opposite edges of everything replaced the middle ground in syncopated rhythm with my mood swings.

This was actually a fair improvement for me over my usual level of holiday cheer. Christmas was always hard in our family. The holiday didn't bring out the best in any of us. We went through the motions: we strung lights and had a tree with obligatory presents under it. We watched Mitch Miller Christmas specials on TV but didn't sing along. Some years we trudged off to midnight mass on Christmas Eve, but that stopped eventually. We all knew how we were supposed to behave, it just wasn't in us to fake it.

Once I was in high school and my older siblings had left home, it devolved quickly. I have a Christmas photo of my mother and me sitting at opposite ends of an avocado-green, Naugahyde couch. My mother was staring at an unopened gift in her lap. Her expression might have been wistful or maybe it was just hollow. I was sitting a hundred miles away, just on the other side of the orange and brown zig-zag afghan, slouched as I looked away, out of frame, an opened gift in my lap. It was a snapshot of our traditional holiday separateness.

My gift that year was a popcorn popper. Mom explained, "You can take it with you. When you leave, it can go wherever you go." Neither of us could wait.

Christmas dinner marked the end of the holiday. Mom always baked a ham and there was pie for dessert. The TV was on in the other room to hide the silence. As soon as we finished, each of us went to our separate corners. Dad was back in his recliner, mom was cleaning up in the kitchen and I was in my room, waiting for time to pass. Every year it was a test and every year we all failed. Once I left home, I never went back for the holidays. Not once.

Out in the real world, I didn't like Christmas any better. Each year friends or lovers would invite me to their family celebrations. Some of the homes tried so hard to cheer the holiday on that I thought the house might explode with the effort of trying to get it right. Some families loved each other loudly and some families were almost as sad and disconnected as mine. I couldn't make myself feel I belonged, even on the fringe. At the end of the evening, the drive home to my dark apartment made me feel awkward and lonely, until my dogs greeted me at the door.

Each year I tried harder to extricate myself from the holiday and each year, well-intentioned friends cajoled, threatened and dragged me back in. Like it would be the worst thing to be alone on the holidays, they fought me to participate and called me Scrooge until I finally gave in to please them. I dressed up and politely arrived on time but I was already counting the minutes until I could leave. At the same time I wondered if this was such a time of joy, why they needed to push the holiday so fiercely. One year a friend's mother actually said, "I know you have *no holiday traditions of your own...*"

Like I was a lost waif without family traditions. That was silly—of course I had holiday traditions passed down in my own family. Ours were not as flamboyant, but they were honest. At that moment, my usual tradition of eating at a delicatessen followed by resting in a cool, dark movie theater seemed more appealing than praising the Swedish flags that decorated her tree. I reminded myself that she might have meant well and checked my watch.

All of this is to say, that whether you love the holiday or not, at a certain point there's a lot of Christmas baggage. Sometimes literally in the form of boxes of decorations and lights for a family pageant that must be acted out, more from habit than desire. Sometimes in the form of hard memories or just not fitting the cultural standard. Sometimes this holiday is like a shoe that doesn't fit, but year after year, like Cinderella's ugly stepsisters, we try our best to force ourselves into it. Sometimes the honest and courageous action is just say, "No thank you, this holiday does not fit me." I did that the Christmas of 1999, my first year on the farm.

Traffic was heavy driving home on Christmas Eve but each mile closer to the farm, there was less traffic and fewer Christmas lights. I stopped at the grocery store and got my favorite foods for the next day, a bottle of wine, and a stack of movies for the VCR. It was almost dusk as I closed the gate. My plan was to not open it again for a few days.

My first stop was the barn. Spirit and Dodger had settled into the quiet prairie life. There was no more worried pacing and their hooves were improving. They nickered low and sweet, and the dogs trailed along as I threw hay. It was bitter cold but my neck got longer as my shoulders dropped low. I did not think about the holiday, or my family, or the relationship I wasn't in. I didn't dwell on resentment about the past or fear about the future. I was here now with good horses and dogs, and I let it be enough.

Chores took forever with long curry breaks during the mucking. Spirit was never much for eye contact, but there's a smell to a horse's mane that is part hay and part dander and part intoxicating dream. My nose pushed deep into his mane and he curled his neck around my shoulders, holding me in the twilight. Later, there was a warm bran mash with apples and carrots and molasses on top, served with love. The act of doing barn chores was like floating in gratitude: the thicker it got, the slower I moved.

Back inside, there was no tree and no cookies left out for Santa. First thing in the morning, the dogs piled on the sofa with me for movies and lazy naps. At mid-day, we strolled in the south pasture with the horses. We let the prairie make us small. There was no need to pace or guard myself, or look for pain to resist. My eyebrows got soft and my belly relaxed. I was here now. Not in some other house where I was the token holiday orphan. Not in a house where I tried to leave early so I could go home to my dogs. Not in a house where I hid in my room, waiting for something bad to happen.

Over the next days, I still felt the pull and push of opposite edges but a rhythm began to emerge in the middle of all the disrepair and mess. Nature set a smooth rolling pattern, sunset to sunset, between chores and financial drama there was moon-light and abundance. In the middle of the plain, flat ground there was a sense of exotic wonder. I felt out of my urban ele-ment, yet as though I had been here forever. The horses in my barn shared the quiet affirmation that had been repeated since the first Christmas in a stable: Peace on Earth. Goodwill to all God's creatures.

Hired Help is Like a Box of Chocolates

Happy New Year. With the gallery closed, I had one burning question: Do they sell mail-order hazmat suits to civilians? Because there was something unholy in the old hen-house: a chalky white powder mixed with the straw, a few inches deep on the floor. When it was disturbed, it rose in the air and hung there like fog for a very long time.

I read somewhere that there was some sort of dread disease carried in chicken manure that killed horses. Or maybe I imagined it. The ex-hen house was a shipping container made with thin plywood walls and held together with metal strapping. There were five or six of these lashed together for storage back behind the barn but they were frayed and curled, a few blizzards worse for wear.

Next to the hen house shipping container was another container that had a hundred or so cans of half-used paint—rusty, frozen, and missing labels of any kind. They actually qualified as toxic waste so I had to have them professionally removed. The material on the floor of the hen house is much worse than paint cans, but outside the law apparently, so I covered myself head to toe with trash bags, found my old swimming goggles, and tied a bandit handkerchief over my nose and mouth.

I was running backwards with my lists. Every time I checked one task off, I added six more. I studied the laws of leverage that stated a woman with a brain could hoist and move an object that four testosterone-driven men would have to grunt loudly and injure themselves to move. I collected a whole slew of leverage devices, like hand trucks and lever spikes and a flotilla of assorted wheel-barrows. Once the shipping containers and dog runs were broken into movable pieces, everything went to the north side of the garage. That's where my very own dumpster resided. Each Tuesday the trash man came and emptied it. It was usually the social high point of the week when I said hello to another human. As soon as he drove the trash truck away, I immediately filled the dumpster up again, packing it tight like a suitcase from the neat pile of waiting trash.

Still, some jobs I had to hire out, and with no one to refer me, I picked up a copy of the local paper. I called a number for a handy-man and he arrived promptly at seven a.m. the next morning to make the bid for building a second small pen. He took measurements and could do math: he seemed competent enough, so I hired him.

Three days later, he and a helper showed up to start building about midday. They took lots of breaks and they were fearless. They squatted down and drank out of small paper bags right in front of me. The pen ran over time and budget, but I have to admit, the lines were straight. After that, I got my bids in the late afternoon, so I could check sobriety.

I had a list of electrical problems and a clothes dryer without a plug. I'm probably capable of understanding electricity, but from the number of times I've had self-inflicted shock therapy from my electric fence, maybe not. I gritted my teeth and made a blind call for an electrician. He arrived in a company van, mature, serious, and very sober. This was more like it. I cheerfully showed him what I needed: A new switch in one room, a light fixture installed in another, and finally, a dryer plug.

But the electrician had a critical eye. My fuse box was bad, and the location for the dryer was bad, along with every inch of wire in the house—bad, very bad. And it was not just the electric, he glared at my dogs and he frowned at my kitchen. I wasn't sure if the work he said I needed was to get my house up to legal code, or if it was some personal code of his own, which I was failing badly.

When he was out at the power pole, he had an especially

big grimace for the horses. He inspected their partially sheared flanks and asked what the stupid clip job was all about. I explained that we sometimes do a partial clip, a trace clip, on a horse that gets heavily worked in the winter, so sweat can dry quicker. He sneered, "I've never heard of anything so stupid, and I've had horses my whole life."

He left me there looking at my horses, "stupid" hanging in the air, as he stalked off to the porch to frown at my dryer. I was paying for this abuse? Why did he feel like he had the right to talk to a stranger this way? It's not like I was family. I could see his silhouette though the porch window. His unhappy profile reminded me of someone. I scoured my mind, and then I recognized him. He was my father, in attitude more than appearance.

Sometimes I wished that my parents could have seen my farm. They would have hated it, but I still wanted their disapproval. It's a hard habit to break. They disapproved of my self-employed career and didn't like me having horses, or anything else for that matter. I was a shining example of everything they disliked, but this would be the biggest insult: trashing their rural-to-suburban victory by moving back; I was still a disappointment.

When I wrote the grumpy electrician a check for his work, I was reminded that not everyone had my vision, understood it, or even wanted to understand it. The sober electrician wanted me demoted from dreamer to white trash. When he finally took his sorry self off to leave, I waved a hearty good bye in the driveway, standing next to the re-purposed bathtub/flower planter.

Next on my list: Repair the ravine by the pond so the horses could use all the pasture. On my particular part of the prairie, there was an overland water system, ponds and streams that trailed along for miles. I don't know the source or how far it went past my farm, but there was a sweet pond where my property and two others intersect on the west side. I was the only one who could see it, so I called it mine.

I learned the history of my ravine just before Christmas. I

was in a feed store checkout line, giving directions for a hay delivery, when the cowboy behind me grumbled, "So you live in that place..." The cowboy told the story. During a storm the pond was rising fast and threatening to flood the house. There was a series of berms built by the Corps of Civil Engineers along this water way, and there was one just to the south of the pond. The previous owner took his back hoe and cut a big hole in the berm, allowing the water to flood his neighbors instead of himself. That might be one reason he decided to sell—the neighbors didn't like him much after that. I almost apologized to the cowboy.

Yes, I bought *that* place. That flood tore out a good stretch of land and carried the soil far away. This time, I picked a card off the board at the feed store: "Man with backhoe, cash only." That usually means hiding income and probably no insurance, along with almost affordable. As far as I could tell, hiring help was a crap shoot that I couldn't win, and I had to get the job done.

Once more, a truck came down the drive to bid a job. This man was clearly retired and in his late sixties. He smiled easily and seemed a bit like someone's weird uncle, but in a good way. After the drunk handyman and the much-too-sober electrician, I hired this guy on the spot. It took him two days of dirt work to get the crevice filled and even with breaks for the tractor and him to cool off, the work still went quickly.

I was working away outside the whole time, dismantling those shipping containers. We chatted some in the course of it—I asked an opinion or two about projects and he had some good ideas. I was feeling strong, dragging wood to the trash pile.

In the process of dismantling the containers, I made a discovery—there was an actual shed structure in the middle of all of these shipping containers. The shed had a roof and two stalls. Livestock had lived there. I brought a sandwich outside and sat down to enjoy my find, and the backhoe man came and joined me with his lunch. He congratulated me. Even with teeth missing, he had a great laugh. He was around the age that my father would have been, I guessed, and so much more pleasant to work around. Then he asked me out.

I suppose if I had been popular in high school, or any time since, I would have had a polite answer. Instead I stared.

How do men end up with this kind of confidence? He had an easy twenty-plus years on me. Should I be flattered? Women almost never have the guts to ask someone young enough to be their son out. Was I proud or depressed about being attractive to large equipment operators? It was almost enough to make me lose my sense of humor about men. Was my midlife crisis having a midlife crisis?

I borrowed some of his courage, and thanked him and begged off. "I'm done with dating," I said. Then I got to hear his laugh one more time.

The garage was next on my list. The home inspector told me it was built over top of half my leach field, which was bad, but it was the most recent construction on the farm and had an actual cement floor. True to the habits of the previous owner, it was unfinished. It had exposed OSB walls, a kind of manufactured particle board that always looks frail to me. I wanted to get siding on it before the prairie wind blew it to bits. One more time I made the call for bids on the job and this time two people came to look. The first handy-man was really congenial. He chatted away like we were old friends, saying the job was straight-forward and easy. The second handyman came out to measure and he was more standoffish. He was a cowboy, and called me "Ma'am." I bit my tongue to keep from calling him "Baby Boy."

The first handyman dropped by the next day with his estimate. As I was reading it, he told me he would give me a discount if I let his hired man move in. I paused my reading and looked up, sure I had misunderstood him.

"I noticed you had a spare bedroom," he said.

My head tilted to the side, like it would be less ludicrous if

I looked at him sideways. Then he told me that he would stand behind his hired man; his guy was a solid, totally trustworthy. He said I could take his word for it. Even if he acted like we had been friends for years, that wasn't actually true. I answered in one word.

"No."

I felt like I had dodged a bullet the first time the cowboy showed up to work, with siding materials and a replacement front door and two windows. He had half the garage done the first day and all of a sudden, "Yes, Ma'am," started to sound like a term of endearment.

In three days, the garage was mostly done, one window was replaced and the front door started. And then he didn't come the fourth day, or the next four days either. Everything was half done, including the installation of the front door. I couldn't get him back out to work. I couldn't even get him on the phone. Now what?

That's when I had the best idea yet. "If I'm going to over-pay for late and shoddy work, why not have the satisfaction of doing it myself?"

Besides, winter was coming and I was getting cynical. I had a few basic tools, and the cowboy left a case of caulking compound. How hard could it be? I started with the front door. It was hung but not finished. I built a frame on the inside. Then I replaced a window. When I didn't have a tool I thought I needed, I used something from my goldsmith workbench. After twenty-five years of building gemstone settings in metal, using hammers, saws, and torches in my daily work, I knew the language. Was replacing a window really that different than setting a gemstone?

The family story goes that my first sentence I ever said was, "I'll do it myself." It might be a charming attitude for a little boy, but not for a little girl. A little girl with an independent streak was likely to be labeled bull-headed before she ever got to school. If that wasn't enough, I was farm-raised. We're a self-sufficient bunch. I quit the Brownies after a month because I thought they were sissies gluing macaroni on paper when there were horses to ride.

My mom was a strange combination of strong and weak. She was emotionally frail and filled with anxiety. At the same time, she could work a farmer's day on top of housework. At one point, she decided that she wanted a corner china cabinet, so she built one with plywood and installed glass in the doors. She stained it dark and displayed china we never used in it. Mom was every man's dream, a woman who worked like a farmhand and was submissive and fearful. She believed life was a vale of tears. And so for her it was.

My parents shared the opinion that men were better by birth, but my father had a special gift. He believed that he had the ability to see stupidity more clearly than average men and it came with the right to point it out. He would have preferred a son when I was born and I grew to share his disappointment that I was not a boy. Even a little girl could see the advantages to being a man.

My dad got me my first horse, and while I was still short enough for the pony to kick me in the face, she did just that. It was the result of a chain reaction. She didn't know I was behind her, in that blind spot that horses share with car drivers. We both startled and my cheek ended up bruised and my ears rang loud, but Dad saw it and yelled at both of us. He stood me in direct kicking range behind her for two more hours. The pony kept a nervous eye on me and I loved her back, joined in punishment. Dad meant to teach me to not be afraid, but I was always more scared of being in front of him than behind a horse. I can't imagine that he ever actually wanted kids, but if they were a necessary evil, his kids would not be weaklings. It was an opinion that, like everything else about Dad, frightened my mother.

His plan backfired in my case. For a man who didn't like feminists, he did a decent job of raising one. Farms are not finishing schools—what did he expect?

Twenty years later while following me through an airport, he muttered, "You walk just like Eleanor Roosevelt." His voice was thick with insult.

I chirped back, "Dad, Eleanor Roosevelt said that no one can make you feel inferior without your own consent."

I think Dad would have liked to watch me install that window. Not that he wouldn't have been critical of the job, but because even now it was still true: *I'll do it myself.*

A Sandbox of Monumental Proportions

It was late February and there were days that the sun felt almost warm. Spirit was back to his old self and Dodger was improving. Not quite sound but much more cheerful, and on a campaign to win over anyone passing by. And best of all, the ground was mostly thawed and we were ready to ride.

First I needed a sandbox of monumental proportions: a riding arena. Footing matters to a performance horse. They need to be able to trust the ground under them for balance and consistency, not to mention the importance of protecting joints and tendons with soft footing. Think of a thousand-pound ballerina on a rocky hillside with gopher holes. But plowing up an area in the pasture is not necessarily the same thing as a riding arena. Raw soil on the Colorado prairie is kind of like chocolate chip cookie dough, while an arena with footing should be more like lemon meringue pie, with a flat hard base and sweet light sand on top. It's complicated dirt.

I re-evaluated my mutating to-do list each day as priorities shifted between what needed demolition and what needed construction. Money flew out of the bank but my one-day-a-week studio was busy. I had work orders coming in and since I no longer had the overhead expenses of my gallery, it appeared that my income was up. Besides, an arena was a necessity. I rearranged the list and plowed ahead. Literally.

First I measured out the standard and legal size for a dressage arena and planted flags on the flat, level land right out front by the road. It was the highest spot with the best drainage, and this way if I came off a horse and got hurt, someone driving by would eventually see me.

I was reluctant to hire the same man who repaired my ravine. A second trip out might constitute a serious relationship. Instead I found someone else with edgier eccentricities and the equipment needed to peel away three inches of prairie grass and topsoil neatly and then pile it into a surprisingly tall mountain of dirt behind my barn.

Hiring heavy machine operators was a whole other level of bizarre beyond hiring a handy-man. I'd never done it before I moved to the farm, but it was certainly the best reason to purchase my very own tractor, skid steer, and back-hoe, even if they each individually cost more than my property. If the job needing done was truly simple, like manure hauling, I could get in and out in fairly sound shape if I paid cash and kept my head down.

Talking about arena footing with these guys was crazy-making. They told me they knew precisely what they were doing, that they do this exact work all the time, and no input from me was required. But I'd listened to too many riders complain about bad results in this complicated process to be very trusting and my horses had been struggling with lameness already. It didn't matter, in the end these machine-loving men thought anything having to do with horses was a return to the dark ages and pretty silly since the advent of dirt bikes that don't eat hay.

Rule number one is that guys who personally own heavy machinery don't fit into a social norm. As a matter of fact, they take pride in being outlaws. They usually wear denim shirts with the sleeves cut off. It might have fit him in high school but certainly not in the decade since then. If they have facial hair from some other century, the degree of communication difficulty will double. It goes without saying that they probably don't share your social concerns or political leanings. And they aren't wild about listening to dilettante women drone on about the precision needed for hacking up a pasture that looked like a dull spot to ride in the first place. It slowly becomes obvious that they own guns and you probably wouldn't be the first woman they've shot at for lipping off.

Rule number two: Choose your words accordingly. I tried to make cheerful suggestions in the form of a question, trying to set him up to look smart. Most girls learn early on how to flatter a man into good behavior, but in this case the usual tricks didn't work and I was worn out ingratiating myself. So I took the high moral ground and bit my tongue.

Once the initial work was done, I had to apply the same verbal acrobatics when the dump trucks arrived with the arena footing. I skipped any attempt at honest communication this time and tried charming each driver into spreading their load as gradually and evenly as possible. One after another, giant dump trucks rolled into the arena and offloaded about ten cubic yards of washed sand at a time. Some drivers agreed, moving slowly along as they dumped their loads, leaving piles that were three or four feet high, but some drivers dumped their load all in one huge pile. I had an opinion about that too, but I could see they wore the sleeveless uniform of heavy equipment operators, so I waved good bye with a forced smile, several thousand dollars less in the bank, and 170 tons of sand piled in my arena.

For all the work they had done, there was at least twice as much still left for me and it felt debilitating considering how much tongue-biting had gone on. At this point it would take a smaller tractor a few hours to level out the piles but I didn't have one. I had to mitigate their unwillingness to dump the sand evenly with a shovel and a rake and a willingness to do it myself. As I began leveling the arena, I imagined a Zen riding garden. It would be a place of beauty and a labor of love, done under the watchful eyes of my beloved and mostly sound horses, and two cynical cattle dogs. All opinions noted, the work began.

I usually started early in the day when it was still cold out and raked until mid-morning. With breakfast at five am, lunch comes before noon. I had developed a siesta habit during the middle part of the day. The horses always napped then and it kept them happy. I thought the countries that practiced the fine art of siesta were much more civilized than we were, or maybe raking tons of sand flat made me think that anyone else was more civilized than I was. It doesn't matter—when I woke up again it was almost like having a new day in the afternoon.

Sometimes to break the monotony of raking, I did a bit more demolition, maybe tearing down another moving container or hauling old tires out of the pasture. Tuesdays came and went; I tried to not appear desperate for company when I rushed out to say hello to the trash man. I scared him a little at first, but he got used to me. I don't think people talked to him much either.

And then of course, I could always rake some more. Finally, the sun got low and it was happy hour. I didn't want to lose whatever thin veneer of urban sophistication I had, so an afternoon cocktail was in order. I usually took a beer and my book of lists out to the barn. I leaned back in the afternoon sun, mentally pondering my lists and resting my back. It was cold out but the sun stayed a bit longer each day. February was letting me know there was hope for more time outside soon, but I still made use of each moment.

The to-do list was adjusted with satisfaction when a project was finished, and another task was added, or more likely, two. Usually I played a mind twister game of planning my work process: on one hand I had my meager resources and on the other hand was what needed to be done. Jobs were big, tools were few, and the labor force was one. With a newfound knowledge of creative physics, I felt stronger and smarter than ever before. The Queen of Recycling and Re-tasking, I ruled over a handful of tools that I mis-used with creative fervor.

Supper was simple, usually a little more of what I had for lunch, washed down with the dregs of my beer. And then back to my arena. Dusk was the best time of day to rake. The light filtered horizontally through the tall prairie grass and I felt an easy gratitude for the day. Leveling was good therapy.

At night I slept honest sleep, dreamless and secure. When my head hit the pillow and the lights went out, the silence of the prairie settled my busy brain to rock-hard peace. Days began to feel timeless; I settled into a routine of familiar work that had simple, obvious benefits. The truth was that I had landed here about as lame and lost as my horses.

By late April the arena was level and we were all stronger and sounder. I'd roll out of bed before dawn and make a quick trip out to the barn to throw a small flake of hay to each of the horses. Back in the house, I brewed my coffee and fed the dogs and cats. Then the very best part of the day: in my pajamas and boots, with a barn coat on top, I made my way back out to the barn. The horses had finished their hay and stood at the gate as the sun was almost at the horizon. The sky was reborn every single morning, colored sometimes with infinite pastel subtlety, and other times, with brash psychedelic color. I took a sip of coffee and opened the gate. My horses, mine, galloped off to the pasture, tails flagged and hooves pounding. They galloped as their ancestors did, in a sprint of thrilling power. A moment later their heads were down grazing and if I squinted my eyes just right, the prairie sunrise could turn an old white horse pink; a rosy glow for a precious moment. Strolling through the pasture I could smell the sage crushed by hooves a moment before. It was impossible to deny how completely the farm owned me.

Change is hard and the details don't really matter; it isn't about good or bad. The expression of each individual day is what matters. The horses go forward and so do I. Maybe years will pass and hindsight will reveal what is not visible today. Maybe I'll be lonely forever and maybe the work will never be done. Maybe I'll fail this farm. All I have is right now; the day starts pink and the rest of the colors are up to me.

The Farm on Leaf River

Maybe it was the daily demolition of the farm or maybe it was the deconstruction caused by my midlife crisis, but memories of my childhood farm came wandering back, images I hadn't thought of in years. When I was a year old, my parents, half-brother, sister and I moved from northern North Dakota to a farm on the Leaf River in central Minnesota. The house had three rooms downstairs. There was a Formica table in the kitchen with a large, white enamel drain-board sink and cold linoleum on the floor. The warmest room was the living room, where the oil furnace was. Dad sat in a platform rocker and there was an old nylon sofa. By the time I was in school, we got a television, complete with one station. In the corner was the door to my parent's bedroom, always closed. Steep stairs led up to the attic in the eaves of the house, split into two bedrooms for us kids. My sister and I shared a bed, and in the winter we'd roll out from under heavy quilts and race down the steps to get dressed by the heater. Dresses were required for girls at school, so we wore pants under our skirts to save our skinny legs from frostbite while waiting for the bus.

Mom had a huge garden in the summer; a couple of acres plowed and planted with potatoes, vegetables and the best melons. There were long rows of raspberry bushes and we sold cucumbers to the pickle factory. As the summer season wore on, the shelves in the root cellar under the house was lined with canned vegetables and berries. Below the shelves, bins were filled with potatoes and squash, and crocks with carrots stuck in sand. There was a trap door in the kitchen and Mom sent me down the dark ladder to fetch potatoes for dinner each night. It was my scariest chore with the musty smell of mold and mice and monsters.

In the early years we had an outhouse situated between two lilac bushes that were so large we had trails through them. Spring was wildly intoxicating after those long, dark winters and nowhere as much as inside those lilacs. We got indoor plumbing in 1960—a bathroom built in a corner of the kitchen meant no more chamber pots. Mom altered the outhouse into a playhouse for me the next spring. We both dreamed of me living away from home from an early age.

My mom tells a "funny" story about returning me to the hospital after I was born. She left me there a couple of months. Living as far from town as we did, I can't imagine she visited often. The "funny" part was why I got returned: I stopped breathing sometimes and she had to hold me by my feet and spank me. I swear it isn't any funnier when she tells it.

Like any good farm, the barn was at least five times the size of the house. We farmed hay and corn for silage, the feed source for cattle that is stored in silos. We had twenty-eight dairy cows, but we were primarily a sheep farm. We leased the farm from the man who owned the car dealership in town. Sometimes he would drive out in his Cadillac and have coffee with my dad. Maybe the car dealer felt a mix of envy and pity for us. He liked us well enough that we got a box of fresh oranges when he came back from his winters in Florida. Once he brought us a pineapple—what a thing!

I'm not sure how old most girls are when they start farming, but I was three or four. I remember the day, standing not waist high between my parents in front of the kitchen sink. Mom was yelling and crying all at once. She told my Dad that she didn't want me in the house with her anymore, she couldn't do it. "You keep her outside with you," she said. It had been a hard few years on the farm; she was recuperating from a bout with cancer. Mom took no joy from her youngest girl and the housework was never done.

Maybe my mother felt she was still being punished for her one great adventure. Growing up with an alcoholic father and a crowd of rough brothers, my mother was used to long hours of women's chores, so when the opportunity came during WWII, she went out to become a welder in the shipyards in Portland, Oregon with her dad and two brothers. It must have been a jolt after farm life. She met a man there, married, and had a son. When her husband turned out to be a womanizing, abusive drunk, she curled up in humiliation for a few months until she finally made a desperate call home and got the money for a divorce and a train ticket back for her and her son.

My mother considered herself lucky to marry my father after that. He was a big improvement; a hard-working man who wasn't a drunk was a catch for a divorced woman in those days. The time in Portland wasn't a secret exactly—my father obviously knew and so did my half-brother. Maybe it was the shame of divorce, but no one told me my mother had been married before. I found out eavesdropping on a phone when I was sixteen.

What maternal energy my mother had was given to her son. She loved him like a suitor, taking his side in every situation, leaving my father feeling like a rival for his wife and my sister and me somewhere beyond that. The animosity escalated between the males in our family and as my half-brother got older, the fights with my father got louder and more violent.

My half-brother hated the farm and couldn't wait to get away. He passed his time torturing animals and dominating me. Six years older, my half-brother bullied me with long-winded threats that included his biggest insult.

"Daddy's favorite, daddy's favorite," he chanted in a high pitched sing-song voice as he blocked me in a corner and leaned over me, air punching to make me flinch. It worked. I always flinched because every few fakes, he'd land an ear-ringing slap or a punch to my stomach. I wasn't exactly sure what favorite meant, but it must be bad.

When my father was mean there was a dark anger behind it, but with my half-brother, it was a sneering smile. He'd hide behind something and when I passed, leap out and give a mighty shove that sent me flying face first into a building or the dirt. My skinned knees and bruised face showed the impact. "Go tattle, little baby," he'd yell at my back as I ran away.

If I went to my mother for help, she'd fuss with her apron and look anxious. "I don't want to hear it, don't you tattle." Her voice got deep when she whispered. She never corrected him. "Your fault," she told me, "You should have stayed out of his way."

I was afraid to tell my father anything, so I hid in the barn. It was safe with the animals, none were as dangerous as my tormentor. I must have looked like a shy, clumsy girl, accident-prone and sullen. With my mother's sheltering defense, my half-brother grew up cruel with a chip on his shoulder, always complaining that the world didn't give him his due. In the end, he was right about that much.

My sister coped in a middle-child sort of way, not making much noise and getting lost in the background. It's a smart plan in a dysfunctional family. She worked in the house with mom and grew up fast under the workload. I have strangely little memory of seeing her. Our parents played us against each other, and we were so different to start with, that we weren't able to help each other much. In line with our family tradition, my sister left home as soon as she could.

Though I was the youngest child, I was certainly not the baby. Right away I noticed that it was a real mistake to be born a girl. Women had all the bad jobs and stayed inside; they got in trouble all the time. Men worked outside with the animals and were the boss. I was strong willed and asked too many questions to get along with the men and I wouldn't stay in the yard or take naps, so being in the house was hard, too. I picked my own way down the middle and ran with the farm dogs.

I left the house at the same time Dad did every morning and wandered away from him at the first opportunity. Dad was always walking fast, always mad about something. He was too busy to watch me so I had the day to myself. I came in for lunch and was out again until dinner. I hadn't started school yet and was no help with heavy tasks, so I dawdled my day away doing animal chores and tried to steer clear of my half-brother. During lambing season it was my job to bottle feed the orphans. I burned the trash, worked in the garden, and took care of the chickens. There are no days off on a dairy farm and milking each of the twenty-eight cows twice a day took some time. Any planting, harvesting, repairing, or any of a million other tasks, happened between milkings.

We had an oil drum at the side of the barn that was always half full of dead animals: lambs that didn't make it, cats that were run over, animals that dad killed for cause. The smell of death was always there. I feared the "dead barrel" worried I would end up there, too.

There were times that my parents needed me out of the way, but there weren't always hands free to keep an eye on me. Folks came each spring to help with sheep shearing and in the flurry of activity, one year I wandered off to play by the river. I was maybe five years old and the waters were high. It's hard to say how I came to be floating down the river, but it probably wasn't an accident. They said I was laughing, clinging to a branch and shooting the rapids by the time Mom noticed I was missing from the spot she left me. I got hung up on a sand bar in the shallows a quarter-mile down the river by the time they arrived to rescue me.

Clearly a better solution was required, so Lady was enlisted as my babysitter. She was a tall, gray mare our family owned. We were already friends. I spent hours loitering in her pen because we liked each other's company. On busy days, I got hoisted up on her back and then my parents were free to work. We stayed in her pen, but she had a rope halter and lead tossed around her neck and I got to ride. Lady would stroll around, as I sat on top dreaming of galloping across green pastures. She was much too tall for me to jump down, and no matter how much I kicked, she would only walk. Lady took care of me; she held me on her warm back and told me stories of brave little girls who loved big gray horses. I loved her with my whole heart forever.

Lady actually had a reputation for being a rank mare. My half-brother tried to bully her into work, but it didn't go well. Lady had more self-respect than that. Maybe she was just a good judge of character; most horses are. After a few times of my half-brother being rubbed off on the barn door or bucked off, Lady actually took a bite of flesh from his shoulder. He came back to the house covered with blood. The more he punished her, the more she punished him. Eventually, he couldn't even catch Lady.

Knowing that part, it was a wonder my parents thought Lady would make a good babysitter, but it was common to let kids ride on truck running boards back then, too. They left me on top of her and as far as I was concerned, there was no question—I was safe because I was so incredibly special to Lady. If she hated everyone but me, then I must be a horse whisperer! I just had the magic, every horse-crazy girl's dream. It was my superhero power.

In hindsight, I was an ordinary kid. Lady wasn't all that unusual either. Most horses do echo their riders' thoughts and emotions. Part of learning to be a good rider is having a positive control over your own emotions. Horses reflect our hearts just as clearly as a reflection in a mirror. My half-brother's aggression was returned to him as impersonally as my love for her embraced me. I clung to Lady's reflection of me; I was better with her than anywhere else. My Dad and my half-brother raged at each other and some of that trickled down to the animals and me. Or maybe no one could remember how to be any other way. I kept to myself, sometimes hiding in the corn crib with the cats or down by the rhubarb patch in the tall grass. My best hours were spent watching Lady graze by the river while I lost time daydreaming of horses.

We only had the farm on Leaf River for eight years. When the wool market fell, we tried to make it work with hogs, but in the end, we failed. It was a battle that we each lost, not as a family but separately, as was our way. We didn't comfort each other.

Our time there ended in a farm auction. I had no warning. One morning the yard around the barn was full of trucks, neighbors and strangers sorting through our belongings. The auctioneer started with the implements and the livestock.

My mother made me stay at the house and Lady was gone before I could say goodbye. My pony, too. Then the household furnishings we couldn't take with us, including my sheepskin teddy bear, were all sold to the highest bidder. I never saw who took the dog.

The farmyard was like a haunted battlefield by the time the auction ended. I scuffed my toes in the dirt out to the barn, too lost to cry. Lady wasn't there to talk it out with. All my barn friends were lost from the farm, even the chickens. The barn was gutted. I wasn't sure what I had done wrong or how I could fix it now. My nine-year-old body moved slowly, thick with a sadness rinsed in defeat. I couldn't imagine I would ever be okay again.

The next morning we packed a few essentials into the station wagon and headed west to Washington State. It was November of 1963, President Kennedy had just been assassinated, and the flags were at half-staff as we drove in silence.

Part Two:

Being Jane Goodall

A Kindred Spirit

Just before I met him, I was volunteering at a therapeutic riding center just so I could sink my nose into a horse's mane and breathe. Just before I met him, I was saving money for a trip to Belize. Just before I met him, my marriage was at a precarious balance.

Some of us just never outgrow horses. It was almost a decade since I had left home and not having a horse was still killing me a little bit every day. Sometimes I rented a horse at a tourist stable to spend an hour or two in the saddle. The rhythmic rocking of his walk loosened my hips and gentled my thoughts. It's a sacred position, being spine to spine with a horse. I didn't need to gallop, I didn't need to separate from the others. It was enough to be in the saddle. I just needed to be held *that* way. Depression always followed the sporadic rides. Not having a horse was like constant PMS, but sometimes it got worse. My life was un*stable*. Just like any horse-crazy girl, I stared at photos and looked at pastures, and wondered how I could make it work.

A friend saw him first. She was at a farm looking at an Arabian stallion and saw a newly weaned appaloosa colt with spots like a Dalmatian dog. She thought I'd like him and that's all the urging it took. My future ex-husband and I drove into a beautiful old farm, not fancy. I met a sweet old cowboy and his bride, lovers and farmers together since they were teenagers. I loved them as much as their horses. We walked around the side of the barn and in a pen all alone was a spotted stud colt as wild-eyed and shy as a deer. He wouldn't let me anywhere near him.

We stood and talked a while and I thanked everyone and said I'd think it over. Then I thought of nothing else. I had my vacation fund, but where would he live, how would I manage it? I did research, I made calls. When I should have been sleeping at night, I plotted and planned. How could I keep him safe and protect him? Would I be able to care for him? Could I survive without him? I didn't want to.

I found a boarding barn that was only forty-five minutes away and the old cowboy delivered him there the next week. The colt arrived in one piece but he had never been led or handled. They slowly maneuvered him down the barn aisle into his twelve-by-twelve foot stall and took his halter off. In moments, we were alone. I had a new set of curries and brushes, not that there was any way to get near him. I stood transfixed. He was manure-stained and skinny. I could see whites all the way around his eyes. And for the first time, I saw through his eyes—abandoned by his herd, bounced along in a trailer and now dumped in a strange place. Alone. Foreign. Defenseless Prey.

Every time I tried to get closer, he retreated. It wasn't the way I'd imagined it at all—anything I tried made him worse. So I stood still with my arms at my sides and said affirmations out loud. It was the only positive action I could think of. Affirmations don't have to be true, they can be wishes or things you want to be true, so I told him he was brave and beautiful. I loved him so much my throat choked my words, I even almost loved me. I named him Spirit, another word for soul. Then I told him he was my horse forever—that I would never let him go.

If he understood me, the idea did not comfort him one bit.

Three hours, and volumes of affirmations later, both of us were breathing easier. He let me touch him for the first time, very lightly, on his shoulder. I was still a long way from getting his halter back on him. I had a passing thought, an acknowledgment really, that one day he would die. It was inevitable. My stomach twisted, convulsed. I thought I might vomit. There was a cold sweat, and tears. Even as I tried to pull myself together and act normal, I knew I was being bat crazy.

A few days later, he was tolerating the halter and with the help of a come-along rope looped around his rump, he was almost capable of walking next to me on a lead. Just a few steps but a nice start, when the vet arrived for Spirit's castration appointment. I'd planned on the surgery at some point but it was required in the boarding contract within the first week. The procedure didn't go perfectly and what didn't hurt him, frightened him even more. It didn't improve Spirit's mood at all and now he needed exercise to keep the swelling down. He was a depressed, miserable colt. Just when being anywhere near me couldn't get much worse, I found his *spot*, that magic spot a horse has that needs to be scratched in a way only a human can do. It was a miracle. We started being friends, just in time for his first birthday.

In the next two years, my marriage ended and we changed barns twice. In the financial fallout of losing my home, there were some very tight months but it was easy to prioritize necessities. I drew a line in front of Spirit and nothing else mattered. I couldn't go back to being without him. Spirit saw me just like Lady had—and knew the best part of me was bigger than my circumstances. He gave me a way to transport myself past people who let me down. Spirit gave me a place to anchor my life, a safe harbor. We found a good trainer and a barn family of people who didn't fit into the real world any more than we did.

When Spirit was five years old, a bunch of us from the barn went to see the Lipizzaners when they came to town. It was a chance to dress up, eat an overpriced meal together, and see some fancy white horses. We complimented one another's personal hygiene and off we went. We were western riders mostly, but I'm sure at some point all of us had seen the *Miracle of the White Stallions,* the Disney movie. The miracle in the movie title refers to the rescue of the Lipizzaners from Austria by General Patton during WWII. To my eyes, the miracle was that horses could dance.

Yes, I knew these horses were the U.S. second-string Lipizzaners, only a traveling troupe, and yes, an exhibition ride was not real dressage. Maybe they weren't perfect, but I didn't care. I was mesmerized, riding my front row seat and taking shallow breaths. What did riding like that feel like in the saddle? I dreamed of those dancing white horses all night long.

The next day, I bolted out to the barn. Spirit was a young horse and my riding was just starting to evolve. I'd like to say we had a solid partnership then, but no, the truth was we were a work in progress. He was a bit contrary, just like me, and we were just starting to find our fit. My head was filled with white stallions as I groomed him. My mind has always been extremely visual so it replayed the Lipizzaner performance effortlessly.

I'm not sure how I cued him that day. Maybe I sat a bit differently in the saddle. I know my energy was high and the vision in my head was crystal clear. As we began to work, Spirit's steps evolved to something else. They were big, soft steps, like the Lipizzaners had taken the night before. When I laughed out loud, the steps got even bigger. His trot threw me up in the air and caught me, slow and exaggerated. His canter was uphill and the speed of a walk. Spirit felt powerful. Invincible. We did a half-pass without knowing its name. And pirouettes—really? Was I dreaming? A friend came into the arena and let out a loud cat call. If I was imagining it, so was she. For the next week, we performed like elite dressage partners. Much above our skill level: it was like a glimpse of a possible future. Then as my memory got less clear, the movements came apart until just a seed remained. Dressage takes a core of training and strength that is much more literal than my imagination. I was left with a memory of riding on air with cues as light as a thought—a kind of feel and finesse that I had never imagined.

Maybe Spirit kept a memory of those rides somewhere inside, too. Maybe my mental images were a bit grandiose, even blindingly literal, but he happily volunteered to dance. And in a few months, Spirit lost every spot he had. My loud Appaloosa's spots faded fast and he was left abruptly solid white. Maybe it was a coincidence. Some Appaloosas do lose their spots as they age. Maybe Spirit liked the way he felt pretending to be a Lipizzaner.

I do know this: Visualization is a respected method used by successful people for achieving a goal. And horses are visual thinkers. They mirror our mental states, from fear to confidence. Equine senses are each so much more acute than humans can imagine. I don't know if horses are psychic but perhaps they read us so quickly and well, that it feels that way. For a little while, Spirit showed me a better way to be with him. From that time on I tried to get back there, to communicate on his level instead of mine.

"It is just like man's vanity and impertinence to call an animal dumb because it is dumb to his dull perceptions." ~Mark Twain

We left our western saddle behind and began working our way up the Dressage levels. Spirit was fun to show, always a crisp and spontaneous ride. His confidence improved year by year, and still, every day was a brand new day. He didn't look like a scared baby anymore but he depended on me, stride by stride, just as I did him. It was hard to tell where one of us stopped and the other started. A road trip to a weekend show in our old trailer was still the best fun.

Five years later when Spirit was twelve, we were at a Dressage competition at a beautiful facility in the pine-covered foothills of Colorado. Our first ride was a fourth level musical freestyle: advanced movements choreographed to music. The warm-up was going well when two women waved us over to the rail. They asked if my horse was a Lipizzaner. Spirit was still running that scam.

"No, he's an Appaloosa." They fought me about it, insisting he was a half-Lipizzaner.

"Nope, he is out of Nifty Sally—nothing but Appaloosa." You have to love a riding discipline that makes a horse so dynamic and strong.

Our ride time came. We halted outside the arena and I signaled for my music. The first dramatic notes called to mind a knight charging off to battle, as I confidently murmured my competition mantra: *I love my horse.*

Every Dressage test begins the same, but feels different. Take a breath and enter the arena at the canter to X, the center mark, and halt to salute the judge. Moving off, split seconds drifted as time stilled and… goosebumps. Spirit felt light and strong. We were bold, the first movement was a series of flying lead changes—complicated work that looked as easy as skipping. Spirit was forward and relaxed, our half-pass was smooth as skating on ice. My smile was so big that my lips stuck on the gums above my teeth. I felt beautiful.

Spirit just got better and better. Each of my breaths said thank you. Time slowed, we consciously and confidently shared this physical moment of utter oneness. We finished our freestyle with a crescendo in the music and an extended canter down the center-line, snout to nose with the judge for our final halt and salute. As I dropped the reins, I leaned low and threw my arms around his neck, so aware of all the miles he had carried me.

I grew up in the shadow of a *National Velvet* dream, riding with a sort of against-all-odds hope. Spirit and I were individually kind of ordinary as horses and riders go, and we both knew it. But together we added up to something so much more than our individual parts and we loved the work of learning. It was his heart that inspired us. Now the two of us were doing a whole lot more than surviving. It's hard to describe how it happens that years of hard reality could find a balance with a heart's dream at one moment in time. Spirit and I got there together.

We walked tall and proud on the way back to the trailer. I wanted to scream, "I told you so!" During our first year of riding, I had five unplanned dismounts from Spirit and a couple of injuries. My trainer shook her head way too many times. People didn't hesitate to tell me to sell Spirit, that he was not the right horse for me. Straight to my face. More than once.

Now, for the perfect part: Back at the trailer, I haltered him and pulled his saddle. As I walked around behind him, I caught a toe, I think. But I didn't fall really; it was more like I catapulted myself into the dirt. I hit the ground with such velocity that people passing stopped to see if I was okay. It wasn't a small lower-level amateur sort of fall, but an elite rider effort: I hit the earth like a pile driver. It knocked my wind out, there was blood on my white breeches, and Spirit's tail covered my face. Did I buck myself off my feet? When I could focus again, I rolled my head to the side and looked up at Spirit. He looked back with curious ears at my face, a few inches from his hind hoof. He didn't stop chewing. Spirit was always happy to help humility find a balance with confidence.

It was a perfect day in a shared life. We didn't know it was our last competitive ride. No one can tell the future.

Lonely for Llamas

My farm was only about ninety minutes from my old neighborhood in Denver, half an hour east of the freeway, past the edge of Colorado Springs housing developments on the eastern prairie. It was the country, but in my mind it didn't seem that far. I thought friends would drive down for dinner all the time. Not that *I* wanted to spend almost three hours of driving for an hour of socializing. That made for a long evening, now that I did the math. So friends didn't just drop in to visit and at the end of the day I had no energy to go past my mail-box. The move got a bit more real with each passing week. Consequences that weren't obvious to me initially played themselves out. I needed a new doctor, a new mechanic. For the number of things that I had to change, I might as well have moved out of state.

Even something as simple as grocery shopping became a question. In Denver, I had a conscience about lettuce. I hated to see it die a slow lonely death in my fridge. Sometimes I ate out with friends at the last minute, sometimes I stopped for fresh fish on the way home. I had the ease of shopping daily. Now the closest store was twenty minutes away and I shopped just a few times a month. Being a finicky eater was a waste of time. If I didn't have an ingredient, it wasn't worth the time to run for it. I bought more canned and frozen foods, and I ate what I had on hand. Eating out was rare and food was less of an art and more a necessity.

Remember Y2K? It was when computers turned over to a new set of date numbers (rolling over to 2000) and there was concern that it would somehow trigger a collapse of the world's computers. It turned out to be an overstated "End of Time" warning, but the news focused on it, and that the number of gun sales rose significantly. The gun debate in Denver, and the country at large, was hot after the recent school shooting in Littleton. But a few miles away in my new county, there was no debate at all. Every other advertisement on TV, billboards, and newspapers all encouraged a gun purchase. I'd moved ninety minutes away, to an entirely different culture.

Living alone in the country with no door locks was just fine, but if my neighbors got whipped into a frenzy of gun purchasing to deal with a computer glitch, I was really in trouble. It took a while to sink in that my local news was different because the people were different. In this rural area, I was probably the only one who didn't own a gun already. I was comfortable with the liberal politics in Denver, but my new county was famous for conservative Christian organizations, several military bases, and lots of ranchers. I'd moved not just geographically but *politically.* I managed to be incognito while driving my truck, but I got looks from under ball cap brims when I gassed up the old Volvo.

Sure, my Denver friends had warned me, some had even been concerned for me, and I laughed it off. It isn't like I had ever been in a political majority anyway. I knew like minds existed here, but where were they? At the first election, I thought I recognized the other Democrat in the county. There was a man with a beard smoking nervously outside my polling place. Who else could he be?

Thinking about the doing something and the actual doing of it are always two different things. My tarnished bravado pushed me on, but at the end of the day the insecurity caught up. I didn't want to whine to friends about being lonely and feeling isolated, so I held my tongue. I moved to the farm for a different life and now that I had it, I got a little paranoid. I needed some new friends.

Why not llamas? Such curious, sweet animals, not like other animals I knew at all. I visited local llama farms and was taken into pens with dozens of llamas that would come around me and peer at my face, sniff my hair, and be so gentle—yet at the same time a bit standoffish, almost like a cat. I was hooked.

I chose two pregnant females from two different breeders, and was given a young male as a bonus. Llamas live in herds and change is always a challenge, so I made sure the llamas all arrived the same day. I picked up the first two in my horse trailer. They were light, quiet travelers; llamas cush when moving, meaning they curl their feet under them and lie down. We arrived at the farm and they stepped out of the trailer and politely looked around.

Bandanna was a lovely Peruvian llama, coal black with a perfect white triangle marking around her neck. Her eyes were huge and thoughtfully curious. She was reserved with a bouncy and elegant gait. I knew she would be the herd leader, her bearing was unmistakable. The young male, Thisby, was a tri-color: black, brown, and white. He was barely nine months old and very shy, but he tried to be casual about it.

My horses, on the other hand, both looked like they might spontaneously combust. Neither had seen a llama before, but I suspect it was the smell that was the big thrill. The horses stood stock still, with their eyes wide and un-blinking, and their knees vibrating in a continuing twitch.

The llamas had a new pen right next door, and we walked past the horses to get there. Dodger stood back with quivering dignity while Spirit followed the llamas along the inside of his fence. His eyes could not look away, he may have even thought they were beautiful, but his knees continued to shake.

That afternoon, the other pregnant female was delivered. Pebbles was white with little black spots all over, a polka-dot sort of llama, and our new herd/family was complete. It would be a few months before the babies came, so we had time to settle in and get familiar with a whole new species—ruminants at that! The girls liked each other right away. I felt like I lived in a zoo. What could be better?

When the llamas had been on the farm a week, I was informed by a rider from the next road over that all horses hated llamas. She was miffed she couldn't ride past my home anymore, now that devil llamas lived here. She said my horses would go nuts. Bigot. As she ranted on, I looked back toward the barn and saw two horses and three llamas laying down sunbathing together.

Every day I haltered Thisby and we went for a walk. He had a confident gait negotiating ditches and crossing logs with no hesitation. I planned a summer of hikes. He was gentle and willing; easier to walk than a dog and much more brave than a young horse would have been. But within that first week, he started to look a bit too quiet. I had no idea how he should be acting, it was just intuition. I watched closer as he stood by the hay, he only went through the motions. He had a bit of hay in his mouth chewing, but I didn't think he was actually consuming it. There was no way to tell if he was drinking, as they all shared a water tub. But the odor of his breath changed. I called the breeder who assured me he was probably fine. I watched him a few more hours, and still didn't think he was okay. Again I called the breeder. "Try to get some fluids in him." I got a syringe and some water with apple juice in it, and gently forced some down his throat. Was he weaker?

As the sun set, the wind kicked up and temperatures dropped. Thisby began shivering and he seemed to lose his balance sometimes. I brought him into the house to keep him warm. I called a very reluctant horse vet who told me he was on his way. I didn't have a llama vet yet, and he was my best chance. In the meantime, I continued to try to give Thisby fluids and he continued to decline. In the middle of the night, I laid his lovely long neck on the floor and he was gone. He didn't struggle or flail about, he just exhaled. He was less than a year old, but it was me that had aged significantly through the night. I called to cancel the vet, and he admitted he hadn't left yet.

"I thought it was probably too late," he said. As if that was reason to not come, as if I should have known better than to call in the first place.

Living on a farm requires a pragmatic approach, even in matters of the heart. I had a deceased llama in my laundry room. There were narrow doorways and I knew I had to get him out of the house while his body was flexible. It took some negotiating, but I pulled his front feet a few inches and then his back feet, slowly sliding his body in an arc through the doorway into the dining room. Poor sweet boy, so graceful in life. I was sorry for my clumsy efforts now. I moved my living room rug to the side, and pulled for the front door. He probably weighed around three hundred pounds. My heart was broken for this gentle animal. Progress was slow but there was no one to call to help me. The dogs held concerned vigil as I continued to drag his body. I propped the front screen door open and wiggled Thisby's shoulders over the threshold and pulled the rest of his body onto the front porch. Then I covered him with a tarp and hoped the coyotes wouldn't find him before dawn.

I didn't know Thisby's cause of death and still had two pregnant llamas outside. Were the girls in danger? When morning came, I called the breeder and then their veterinarian who specialized in llamas. I got better answers, but still both assured me that this *never* happens. I could see Thisby's body on the porch. The vet wanted to do a necropsy and I agreed to get the body to her office as soon as possible.

My recent experience of moving heavy objects by myself got put to the test again. Thisby's body was stiff now and I needed to get it in my truck bed. I cried for Thisby and I cried for me. I brought this young boy here and he was dead. While I cried, I made a plan.

I backed the truck up to the front porch. I dragged a piece of plywood from the garage and made a bridge from the porch to the bed of my truck. I sat down on the plywood with my back to the truck cab and pulled Thisby a couple of inches closer to me. I didn't let myself look at his face and forced myself to continue. Then I walked my seat bones back a few inches and I set my fingers into his soft wool. Such a short life. I pulled him a few more inches toward my lap. Crying and scooting, he came along inch by inch onto my lap again and again. Eventually he was in the truck and I was all cried out.

The necropsy results came back: Thisby died of an incredibly rare digestive condition. No one could have saved him, he was doomed from birth. Everyone marveled that it happened with my first llama, and old timers told me it never happens. But it did happen, and it was the first death on my new farm. I knew it would not be the last. I was baptized.

Later that day, Thisby's breeders pulled into my driveway with a trailer on back. They had talked to the vet and knew what happened. There were hugs and more tears, they were so sorry for my loss, such sad news. And they offloaded a lovely black llama with white spats on his front feet. Would I accept this llama in his place?

My heart wasn't in it but the black llama stepped toward me and extended his nose to smell my breath. Horses do that, it's a universal greeting, gentle and intimate. I can recognize friends when I see them, like this llama, like this couple. They were so kind, so generous; it was more than a business for them.

I named him Sebastian and soon our hikes began, this time with a pack that held lunch and water and usually a good book. He protected the farm from coyotes and stray dogs. Llamas are very territorial. We went to llama club activities and participated in llama agility. He especially liked women with red hair.

For the first few months until Sebastian was old enough to be neutered, he had to live apart from the girls. Llamas are very social animals and it was just over a pipe fence, but it felt like isolation. He paced the fence line with a sad moan of an exhale. I could relate.

A neighbor who lived down my road had started asking me for help with her horse. That next week she stopped by to see the llamas, and told me she was going to get a pair of goats the next day to keep her gelding company. Probably a good idea; her horse was pretty sad.

I went along thinking a goat would be good company for Sebastian. Kids come in twins usually. There was a pair of neutered Nubian-cross kid goats who liked me, so Elvis and Sumo joined the family. At the beginning, the kid goats had to be bottle fed a few times a day. My neighbor left her two goats with me since she had long work days. Within a week of getting them, my neighbor announced she didn't want her twins. I was kind of happy for the goats, but I'm sure her horse would have liked a new home as well.

I called the goat breeder and she agreed to take my neighbor's twins back, but by the time I drove them back to the goat farm, all three of us traveling in the cab of my truck, they had talked me out of it. The goat breeder gave me a bunch of free milk and sent me back home. Just Joe and Barney Goat officially joined the family. It might have been their plan all along.

The four kids stayed with Sebastian except for mealtime, when they followed me into the house to heat their milk. After Thisby, I got in the habit of bringing healthy animals in the house, on the off chance I would need to if they got sick. This turned out to be not such a good idea with goats. Soon the kids were jumping on kitchen counters and falling into the toilet, just generally running amok. Gravity barely works on goats anyway, but the day they ate the ornamental wreath above my bed, I decided it had to stop. They could wait for their lunch outside. They stood at the front door and bleated, but I held firm.

Instead, I began a happy hour compromise. I took a beer out to the goat pen and sat down on the tire in late afternoon. They chewed on my hair and played with my zipper pulls. One day they got my tennis shoe off and ate the shoelace. Then one day it happened: I was admiring Elvis' profile and I heard a burp. He looked mildly bewildered, then one of his cheeks puffed out and his jaw set to work. Ruminants have a charming way of barfing up their last meal, or cud, and chewing away at it one more time. I think I got to see Elvis with his first cud.

When I called, "Goatees!" they all came running, bleating loudly and scurrying along in their stiff-legged trot the whole way. Goats aren't for everyone. They are extremists. Narcissists who live to please themselves, without a fleeting thought of anyone else. Kind of like a bad boyfriend. In other words, they were a help with some of the demolition I was doing, if I had any luck aiming them. Then I loaded up the debris into the bed of my truck to haul to my dumpster. The kids would bounce up to the truck bed, then the roof of my cab and finally to the hood which was the best place to watch me drive. As I unloaded it piece by piece at the dumpster, the unending game of King of the Mountain started. They took turns pushing each other off the highest piece of trash. Of course the piece of trash that is highest is also the one on top, so unloading had to be a well-timed event, in between head butts and leaps in the air.

The second spring on the farm the crias arrived. Llama babies are called cria and we had two on the way. The gestation time for llamas is 350 days. Most cria are born in the morning so the sun has time to dry them off. It's a holdover from their ancestors in the Andes Mountains where a night birth was certain death. Each morning I took a special look for anything that looked remotely like labor. The llama girls are very stoic and their wool was long enough to give nothing away.

Spirit usually knows what is going on before me. One morning he paced the fence line of the llama pen for an hour, and then came to a stop with his head though the fence panel. He waited. During our years at boarding barns, Spirit usually had a cat or two in his stall. He shared his grain, and let them sleep on his back and swing from his tail. Now he was watching the llama girls so intently, it could only mean one thing. He was courting a new pet.

Llamas are fastidious animals. There is only one poop pile

and everyone uses it like a family bathroom. That is where I found the first cria, right on top. Maybe Bandanna thought she was having the worst constipation ever; it would be an easy mistake to make. I missed the birth but an impossibly clean baby was right on top the pile. She weighed a healthy twenty-eight pounds and was all bone and hair with very large ears on top. With knee joints bigger than her toes, and a totally out of control neck, she managed to her feet and wobbled haltingly over to where her mom was eating.

The cria kept trying to get in the right position to nurse while the mom seemed distracted and uninterested in her progeny. But the cria finally managed to latch on and almost as an afterthought, the llama mom seemed to remember her. Spirit had been peering through the fence panel for two hours by now. I thought he would have left for breakfast, but he stayed. A few minutes later the llama baby wobbled her way over to the poop pile and relieved herself for the first time. She was born knowing where to eat and where to poop, and she was a strong girl.

Prey animals, like llamas and horses, have to be born on the run. They might have a day or two of relative safety, but they need their survival skills very soon. Predators, like big cats, wolves, and humans, are born more frail. We need protection longer, some of us years.

But there was this brave little cria heart being greeted by the rest of the herd like a precious treasure. We named her Belle Starr, the Outlaw Queen. Spirit and I were that impressed.

A few hours passed and still Spirit never took his eyes off Belle, he was so drawn to her. He stood with his head through the fence panel in a passive pose, quiet and hopeful. Eventually, it happened. Belle made her way toward Spirit. He stayed stock still while she careened and wobbled her way toward the fence. She stopped, all four legs braced at splayed angles. When she was ready, she leaned her little nose toward him and took a tiny sniff as he exhaled slowly. The friendship was sealed in that moment.

From that day on, they met at the fence line for a daily stroll; Belle in the llama pen and Spirit on the other side. I threw hay next to the each side of the fence so the two of them could eat together. A few months later when it was time to wean Belle, the choice was obvious. I brought her into the horse pen. She didn't seem to miss her mom but she stayed close to Spirit. He guarded her like a treasure, even protecting her from the wind.

A few weeks later, Spirit and I were giving a friend's pre-teen daughter a riding lesson on a Saturday morning. We finished and came back to the barn to un-tack when the young rider heard the hum and called, "There's something was wrong with your llama." I went to investigate as it was almost five weeks past her due date. The llamas don't check the calendar like I did and I had about given up. Pebbles was standing with the baby partly born, front feet and head dangling in the air. From this angle the baby could clear his afterbirth and breathe. Mom was humming and baby, still half-born, hummed back, like a soft sing-song call and response.

We did what seemed right. I made the traditional cowgirl lunch of tomato sandwiches and we pulled some lawn chairs beside the pen. We ate lunch and respectfully watched the second half of the birth. Mom and baby took their time, quietly humming back and forth, and finally the long skinny cria swooshed the rest of the way out. The towels were ready and we dried him off under mom's passive eye. The baby stood in a few minutes and joined her mom for lunch, under Spirit's watchful eye. Belle and Bandanna were nearby, curious and quiet. Sebastian had been neutered by now, so he was included in the llama herd. They all stood in a circle to welcome the new life.

The routine settled into place and the llamas became the official greeters, running down the driveway every time someone was at the front gate. There was always a lot of excitement when we had to break in new delivery guys, who needed to be reminded a few time that llamas don't have teeth on top and can't bite. It doesn't help that the llamas insist on standing nose to nose with the delivery guys while I repeat the warning. They stayed busy chasing dogs and coyotes off the property, and let me know if there were intruders lurking. The horses and llamas shared the pasture, grazing side by side. Lazy days passed and when the horses stretched out for a nap, llamas cushed down close by. The goats joined them and we were an inclusive, multi-species nap sort of family.

Sometimes around dusk when the prairie grass was back-lit to a shiny horizontal ebb and flow, and the air was full of pond smells and birdsong—when the time was just right—the llamas queued up. The matriarch would lead, or sometimes one of the cria, but they would arrange themselves by height and bound off in a huge circle around the house, lap after lap. Not the usual trot or canter, this gait was a hopping bounce. If their movement had been a sound bubble, it would have said "Boing!" It was a dignified line with necks tall and ears back, all in the air springing together on the same stride. It looked exotic and primal— like a twilight line dance to seal the day.

Barn Royalty

Spirit was five when Dodger came to live with us. I was riding six days a week, taking at least two lessons a week and competing, but it wasn't nearly enough for me. My heart had grown larger and I wanted a second horse. At first I worried that Spirit would be jealous. I introduced them over the fence first. There were no squeals or ear-pins, so I turned them out in the arena to have a full body sniff. The arched their necks and in a moment started grooming each other. Little nibbles on the neck, a quick bit of trotting around. They acted like long-lost brothers. Spirit was not jealous at all, if anything he seemed relieved. Apparently standing in the blinding light of my love was exhausting.

The very first thing to know about Dodger is that he came from an outstanding family of Arabian horses. His famous grand-sire, WitezII, escaped the Second World War with Patton and the Lipizzaners. His dam was Royal Zara, a Supreme Legion of Merit mare and pretty special herself. He came from a much more illustrious family than the rest of us put together and it was crazy luck that I got him. Working with him was intimidating in the beginning. He was pretty. I mean distractingly pretty and he had intelligence to match. Even just standing next to him, it was easy to feel inadequate. There was an unspoken expectation about him. And me. They did not match.

Dodger was just over a year old. I was aware of my short-comings when I started Spirit, so I had a puffed-up prideful agenda to right all the mistakes I made before. And Dodger was easy at the beginning. There was a bridge obstacle that had been a three-hour challenge for Spirit at this age. Dodger walked over it first try. So I asked him to back over it, and again, no issue. The two horses could not have been more different from the start.

Two years later, I nervously rode my proud and extremely green gelding outside of the arena for the first time. I was confident in my negative thinking; I feared the worst as we strolled around the barn-yard. My sit-bones were stilted in the saddle. I didn't trust him to carry me out loose in the world, worried that the wind would kick up or that dogs would run at us. Maybe a satellite would fall from the sky.

Sure enough Dodger spooked big, staring at a spot on the ground in front of him. I tensed and leaned forward to see what had scared him, totally affirming that he was right to be frightened. He kept staring and so did I. I asked him to move to the side so I could have a better view, and then in our new position he stared at a different place on the ground but even more nervously. Nothing was visible: no plastic bag, no snake, nothing but dirt. Now I was hooked, what *was* he looking at? Eventually I saw it. There was something in his shadow that he hadn't seen before… it was me sitting on his back. Not our most proud moment. I didn't tell anyone. After all, I had been afraid of my own shadow, too.

Dodger and I began training all of the basic work usually asked of young horses. His mind was quick, always looking for action. It worked like a cue on me; I was always on guard. Together we were tense and a little spooky. It seems there is a difference between knowing that a horse mirrors your emotions and actually being able to control your emotions.

I had a hard time connecting with Dodger when he was young, as we were always a few degrees off. I rode Spirit in my lessons and my trainer wanted it that way. She wasn't wild about Dodger at first and the advanced work Spirit and I were learning held my attention. After Spirit and I were done, I passed the leftovers on down to Dodger. He lived in Spirit's shadow, by

Spirit's choice and my passive agreement.

Then Spirit came apart. He got so resistant under saddle that I didn't recognize him. One day he got mad and flipped his head back far enough to whack me in the forehead. My trainer thought the resistance was mental and told me to push him past it. He showed no lameness so I took her advice. But his mood got darker, rides didn't improve and my doubts about his behavior grew. I called my vet and she suggested stall rest for a few days. When she came out a few days later he had a serious limp on his front left leg. It was an improvement, because it meant he wasn't crazy. The vet palpated him and asked me bring him in to the clinic for x-rays and ultrasound for a better diagnosis.

As soon as Spirit started limping, his sweet old self came back. Spirit was a stoic horse. He was no quitter; if I asked, he said yes. The tests showed a serious tendon injury and it didn't look fresh. He had soldiered on. The more it hurt, the more his mood changed, but he hadn't shown me the courtesy of a limp. It was right there, I just didn't understand what he was telling me.

For the next two years, Spirit was on stall rest. Two entire heartbreaking years. He became depressed and wouldn't let me groom him. He wouldn't make eye contact with me. Every time I took Dodger out to ride, he turned his back. Spirit was only eight years old. There was no way to explain this false separation so I took the blame.

That's how Dodger got promoted to first string. I'm not sure when it would have happened if Spirit stayed sound. Riding Dodger felt a bit like detention in the beginning. I didn't think Dodger and I would make it. I had had some success with Spirit but whatever vague confidence Spirit gave me, didn't carry over to Dodger. He was so sensitive that if a trash can was out of place he tensed up and jumped sideways. Or maybe it was me. Competing at lower level dressage was a disaster. Neither of us could focus. Dodger spooked at the letters that were always in the same place. I felt stiff and awkward. Instead of the feeling of oneness, I felt like a box of rocks. No one congratulated us and more than once my trainer spoke through a clenched jaw, "Couldn't you tell he was running off with you?" Yes. I could tell. I just couldn't do anything to save us.

It was embarrassing and frustrating but then when I least expected it, we would have a great movement. Sometimes during a canter, for an instant there were strides that were so elegant and correct that it took my breath away. Then he bolted, tossing his head and flagging his tail. It was almost as if doing correct work set him off. I missed Spirit. He filled in for me if I fell short. Riding Dodger was too hard.

Improvement was painfully slow and gradual, because it was me that had to change. In the beginning I didn't know that. I was too busy blaming him to notice me. I was frustrated that he wasn't more like Spirit. The more I asked, the louder the cues were, and the worse Dodger reacted. I wanted him to partner with me but Dodger had a higher definition of the concept. He needed his opinion acknowledged.

During a hard ride, I gave in by accident. Exhaustion slowed my thoughts down and he slowed right along with me. He rewarded me for not fighting and I heard it. As I thought slower, I became more aware of what the individual parts of my body were inadvertently cuing. When something unexpected happened, I rewound my memory back to the beginning, and I saw that I had actually asked for the problem.

This awareness changed everything because it meant that Dodger was obedient, maybe a little too obedient, and I couldn't punish him for that. I started rewarding him for doing what I asked, even if I asked for the wrong thing by mistake. My ego had to sit down and shut up; I was the problem. His antics in the show ring were my insecurities and panic played out on the big screen. The struggles he seemed to have in training were entirely mine; he just gave an honest response. The more I asked in a positive way, the more he had to give.

It sounds easy enough, but positive reinforcement wasn't

something I learned at home. Once I stopped being even mentally adversarial, he offered a connection so close that he seemed to welcome me inside his skin. I began to hear his voice in my head. Yes, I know how that sounds.

It's actually simple. Here's how to tell if your horse is talking to you. If the first words you hear sound like something *you* would say, like "I want a new saddle pad that's midnight blue with gold trim and then I will take the canter cue," it probably isn't your horse speaking. Settle and breathe and let there be dead air. If you hear something more like, "Hey, do you have to do that with your hands? Well, stop it!" then it's probably him and he's probably right.

It isn't being psychic; listening to horses is a combination of body language, understanding, and mental openness. I was always good at it, and my usual stuff worked with everybody but Dodger. I thought he was scattered, and maybe worse. Truth was that I was a bit slow-witted for him. He thought I was well-intentioned but boring. And that it would be a help if I understood Latin. Dodger had a dry sense of humor.

Does this sound like some sort of horse-crazy talk? Probably so. It's probably a coincidence that the next year we were fantastic. We took to more complicated work with ease, both of us. No more spooking, no more bolting. Each time we halted at X and began a dressage test, we were both totally, wondrously present in the moment. All I had to do was keep up and try to act cool. Where Spirit and I were mentally alike, Dodger and I were polar opposites. He was proud and outgoing. He came by his arrogance honestly—he was born to it. Baby talk and cuddling were beneath him. If I gave him an apple as a treat, he took a few human-sized bites and walked away. His physical appearance was impeccable, he never even got muddy. It was a high standard that he maintained for himself and his rider, and I worked to fulfill his expectations of me.

Dodger loved the precision of Dressage and as I improved, even that got better. He celebrated the details as we trained more difficult movements, since he seemed to know it would add to his cachet. Arabians are a breed that aren't all that popular in dressage, especially at the more advanced levels, but Dodger had long since won over my dressage instructor and was making inroads on the rest of the world. I watched him work his magic on clinicians and Olympic competitors that we studied with; no one escaped his blunt virtue. Dodger had a quality of intelligent ease about him that encouraged the rest of us to be a little smarter.

Every summer my Dressage chapter put on a large show over the Fourth of July weekend. I was president the year we managed to land a pretty important and well-known judge and the show filled quickly. All the planning work was done, the grounds were beautiful, and Dodger and I were set to compete.

Then the judge arrived in such a foul temper that we felt scolded for saying hello. The most we could manage was to stare at our shoes as she showed clear disappointment with every effort we made for her comfort. Worst of all, she was brutal in her scoring. Lots of competitors were angry or in tears with harsh comments and low scores. A few riders got disqualified. People looked to me, but I had no idea how to fix anything.

Dodger and I were competing at Third Level at that point, and our first ride was scored badly. There were no big mistakes, so we rallied an hour later and gave a strong showing at our freestyle. That score was almost twenty points lower than we had ever been judged. During the lunch break the judge passed me and she made eye contact, "The worst freestyle I have ever seen," she said with lips that barely moved. A little over the top to be so personal.

Everyone's morale was miserable. Competitors were unhappy, volunteers were stressed out and quite a few riders had scratched. If the judge noticed the destruction in her wake, it was fine with her. She seemed to find all of us far beneath her consideration. Generally, dressage is a very friendly environment. Because the sport is somewhat cerebral, you rarely see this sort of negativity on either side. It was as rare as a bar fight between librarians and accountants.

By Sunday afternoon, the schedule of rides was light. More than a few riders had scratched their rides and gone home already. Dressage never got many spectators, but now there was a small group of riders who watched the scoring and grumbled. Dodger and I were scheduled mid-afternoon but I was deflated. What a disaster. Dodger and I rode through blizzards and windstorms, always proud that we didn't let externals get to us, but this was a giant emotional challenge. I thought about scratching, or riding to X, dismounting, and flipping off the judge. She inspired that level of sportsmanship.

We went through the motions of warming up, but I couldn't focus, my shoulders slumped. We were called into the arena and trotted to X to salute to the judge. I took a breath and considered my options, still not committed. And I felt my legs widen just a bit as Dodger took a deeper breath. The reins got lighter as he arched his neck a little more and I heard Dodger's voice in my head. "Let me take this one." I hesitated and he continued, "Let's ride down her throat." He said it cheerfully.

Dodger moved forward and this time it was me who made eye contact with the judge. Dodger did the work. I prepared him minimally for each movement and he puffed his important self up. Our transitions were sweet, the extensions bold and hot, and the lateral work was effortless. By the final halt, I forgot all about the weekend, and was breathless and smitten by my brave horse's heart. The small crowd in the stands erupted into applause. At some point a few more onlookers came to the rail and joined in. It was an actual ovation and Dodger was positively strutting out of the arena on a loose rein. He was filled with self-esteem and I had to sit a bit taller just to be with him. We were roundly congratulated and our score was the lowest yet. I could hear Dodger's opinion on the scoring: "So what!" He was a positive affirmation every ride. Have I mentioned Dodger's registered name? It's Royyal T. Say it fast.

There were so many times over the years I was aware that being owned by me limited Dodger but never more than after this move. What was I doing with an upper level dressage horse on this ratty little farm. Was it the end? With no trainer, no barn support, just off by ourselves, were we done? The first few months Dodger pouted, but slowly I started to see my old prince back again. We didn't have help so we listened to each other. Our work improved surprisingly quickly. There was no one to see it, no scores to prove it, but we didn't need that anymore. The kind of thrill we got from the show ring was our everyday ride. We made upper level work look easy. Dodger gave me his confidence. It wasn't that he trusted me more, but that I finally felt as strong and solid as he did. I became extraordinary, too.

He Told Me He Was Ernest

My first actual friend in the new neighborhood was a woman who lived down the road and around the corner, next door to the llama-hating woman, but she couldn't wait to introduce her horses to everyone here. We had very different backgrounds and lifestyles, but we had that one giant passion in common—we talked horses. Within a few months, she and her family moved an hour away to land in the mountains but the bond was set. I got a call from her one Saturday morning. She'd hauled some belongings to her extended family in Iowa in her horse trailer and then the next day went to look at a horse she'd heard about at an auction. She never saw the horse because she got stuck at a small pen of equally small donkeys. They were neglect cases, all very frightened and huddled tight together. Their un-trimmed hooves grew forward like Aladdin slippers, painful to look at. The little donkeys were a teetering, unbalanced herd with wild eyes, steel wool for hair, and a very clear dislike of people.

Naturally she called me to help rescue them. Horse-friends do that. I sent all the money I had just then, not quite two hundred dollars, and she got all four donkeys. That probably means she barely beat the killer bid in auction with a bit left over for initial vet care and traveling papers.

When they arrived at my farm after twelve hours of driving, the donkeys looked wide-eyed and exhausted. I'm sure none of them had rested in days. At least one of them had diarrhea but it was impossible to tell which one. Manure was everywhere. They were a tiny mess. Our idea was to let them stretch their legs and take a break. She backed her trailer up to the gate of my pen and we opened the door. In a few moments one little pair of long ears cautiously looked at the surroundings, and another pair peeked. Then in an instant all of them bolted out into the pen. Immediately one of them dropped with a solid thud and rolled. As if on cue, the rest plopped down onto the ground. They wiggled on their backs and their tiny hooves flailed about in the air, and with a jerk, they leaped up to their feet again. And dropped down again. And leaped up again—a dirt bath is a miracle cure for donkeys. They seemed to think it was the best way to get the stink of humans off, but this group was especially zealous. One by one, they drank some water and then rolled some more. It was like badly-timed donkey calisthenics. They sent up a decent dust cloud to prove how serious they were. The more dust in the air, the less nervous they all looked. Was the sky falling? So they all dropped and rolled a few more times.

This little group all had coarse dry hair and big bellies, but skinny necks and backsides. Donkeys are easy keepers. It would take some serious neglect to look this bad. Three of them were a bit taller and stuck together, excluding the smallest who was also the most skittish.

"Why don't you keep the little one here and work with him? He's going to need some extra time," my friend said. Against the odds, the other three jumped back into her trailer with a little encouragement and some fresh hay. And they left for the final hour of their journey to the mountains.

The donkey left in my pen showed no interest in the fact that the rest of his herd left. He showed even less interest in me.

"That's okay. There's time, little one."

He turned his head and told me plainly his name was Ernest and he was deathly serious.

"Of course it is," I said.

It was undeniable—this nearly crippled little life was proud.

My horses stood all this time in an adjoining pen, watching. Spirit couldn't take his eyes off the little donkey. Now Ernest walked over to the fence and extended his nose to Spirit. I waited for the prerequisite squeal. None. The two of them shared breath back and forth, reaching through the fence panels. It's never smart to throw strange animals together right away. Still I opened the gate and Spirit walked through, leaving Dodger in the other pen. The horse and the donkey stood close and shared some hay. Ernest rested his tired body against Spirit's shoulder. Just like that, it was all over but the tattoos.

Ernest was 36" tall and the Iowa vet guessed his age to be about two. His hooves were so overgrown that it would take months to get him sound and balanced. We needed to get that process started, but at the same time, I had to work very slowly. He required it, he had had enough fighting in his past; he would not tolerate any more man-handling. It made perfect sense. All the force my parents used didn't get a happy answer out of me. I had that same shut-down tension most of my life. I took a deep breath for both of us and I asked him to volunteer. Sounds crazy, but it had to be his idea. It was going to be a slow process.

Sometimes I carried the halter and spent an hour negotiating my feet to a place closer to his feet. I asked for his eye and if he looked at me, I said, "Good boy," and walked away. I spent time *not* catching him. I made myself more interesting that way. Some days I got close and put one hand briefly on his shoulder and walked off. When he finally believed that I meant no harm, that I knew how to listen, he allowed the halter. I never pulled the lead rope and he walked beside me in a dignified small stride. Mutual respect might have been the biggest lesson for both of us.

When haltering got easier, grooming began. A curry comb should be an itchy donkey's best friend but Ernest was tense and nervous. He would not tolerate touch near his shoulders or back. My friend had told me she'd seen an adult man ride him—correction: I meant to say a full-grown man. I save the title "adult" for someone who doesn't make a joke out of frightening an animal.

Ernest had a bit of a sway to his spine and when I stood beside him with a slight lean toward his back, he would spin his hind end away and face me with wide eyes and braced front legs. He was terrified without me touching him at all. That kind of fear is inspired by pain, and being nervous about me was only common sense for Ernest.

After all my years with horses, donkeys were totally different creatures—Ernest gave the master class in what that meant. He was so very smart and at the same time, more primitive. He always listened to his own best counsel. A donkey has the sense to not come out of a barn if there is lightning. Ernest let me know that with donkeys there was really only one question: "Do I trust you?" If the answer was yes, they would give you their foot or any other task you ask. Without trust, they weren't likely to budge an inch. To the insensitive handler, they might appear stubborn, but they believe in civil discourse and polite manners. Appearing stubborn is just their response to rudeness.

Ernest taught me that donkeys are gentle, self-effacing and so very intelligent. A human has to pay the price of admission— they must be trust-*worthy*. Donkeys don't respond to bullying because anger and name calling is the last resort of a lesser species. I definitely wanted him in my barn family. He gave us a little more class.

At the same time, Ernest was extremely playful—much more so than any of the dogs. If I got up at night for a glass of water, I always looked out to check on the pen. Many times I saw Spirit and Ernest wrestling and playing in the moonlight. Ernest would stand up on his hind legs and chew on Spirit's withers or trot next to Spirit with his little neck arched, nipping at Spirit's legs. Spirit was fairly arthritic when Ernest came to the farm. With all the night games, he was soon moving better than ever. Maybe Ernest's real name should have been Chondroitin.

Ernest was a contradiction with hooves and whatever I knew about horses was insignificant in the face of his long ears. He didn't do the sort of hero worship my geldings did—coming when I called and then asking to be scratched. I loved that about

Ernest, he played hard to get. Any interaction required his total permission. He volunteered or he refused with no gray area. This is the place most sensible people gave up, but the challenge to be more eloquent in training intrigued me. My father had told me that growing up, he used a two by-four to train horses and mules. I thought I could do better.

The truth is I probably had a bit of donkey in me. If one of us was stubborn, it might have been me. I was only too aware of the line between patience and force. We did it his way—I worked slowly and did more listening than training.

We started grooming. If anything felt good, he certainly didn't let me know. Each curry circle, each brush stroke seemed painful—especially anything to do with his face. Those long hooves affected his balance and that impacted his security. I knew the farrier was not going to be incredibly patient and Ernest's opinion on that was obvious, so we got to work. I picked up his foot quietly and held it just an instant and set it down. Good Boy! But if he pulled his hoof away, I relaxed my arm and held on while being very careful to not pull back. There was no sense in punishing him for his memory, I just worked on creating a new one. When he quit pulling, I gently put the hoof down. Good Boy!

We worked in very short sessions and I did a lot of scratching. Then we repeated the whole thing a few hours later—into the pen with a brush and curry, and then back out. In the past getting caught meant something bad for Ernest and we needed plenty of happy catch-and-release experiences.

Ernest would submit at best, but we were nowhere near volunteering yet. Slowly we started groundwork—leading, obstacles, and just generally moving around together. Lots of trainers carry whips, not for punishment but to use like a pointer, touching but never close to hurting the animals. If there was a whip nearby, Ernest would refuse to do anything at all. That included breathing, too. It was like he heard an air raid siren—he flinched and froze. He was telling me that he had been pushed hard and shutting down was his response. I tried treats for good work but he didn't trust taking it from my hand. At the end of our sessions, I put a treat on the ground and stepped back. The space between us was a deceptively huge gap.

Everyone had a job here at the farm and abused donkeys were no different. Work heals, I knew it firsthand, so a few months later I mailed away for a training harness. I moved in slow motion putting it on Ernest, especially the over the back and belly parts. He was extremely reluctant but I didn't give him anything to push against. Slow and soft, I stopped and started again. I refused to create resistance on my end, always with a happy voice and a Good Boy! When the harness was on and he was between the lines, I asked for one step. I remembered photos of mules pulling a plow in fields back before there were tractors and knew my ancestors had stood in this sacred place.

Again, I asked him to walk on and he did so at a cheerful pace. Followed by an ask for a halt and yes, a prompt answer. Who was this donkey? I asked lightly for one step back to disengage his movement and he did exactly that. It was a turning point. I did a lot of ground driving when I started horses in training, so the driving wasn't new to me but his response was unusual. Ernest's ears were up and he was marching. Did I feel his chest puff out just a bit?

In a couple of weeks, Ernest got slow. It felt like we hit some sort of resistance. It was easy work, had I over-challenged him and asked for too much? I got a counter-intuitive idea, probably from him, to leave the property and head down the road. It worked like a charm and when we got about a quarter-mile away, a whole herd of horses came galloping to the fence line. A young horse would have gotten caught up in the excitement and come apart, but not Ernest. He didn't even favor them with a glance. He marched on with dignity and I tried to keep up.

Soon we were dragging a tire behind us and not long after that we got a cart. Now we could go hill-and-dale over the property and down the road. We hooked up to go get the mail—the mailbox was a bit frightening, looming over Ernest's ears. We drove through mud-puddles and over tarps and his courage grew.

The next year, we started going to donkey and mule shows. Ernest didn't do so well in the conformation classes. He wasn't very pretty. We did excel at the obstacle driving. It was more challenging and required better communication. After quite a few big wins, I decided to stop referring to Ernest as a rescue. He had earned the right to be an equal there, not a charity case.

My proudest moment with Ernest was at a draft horse show. Some donkeys were invited to do a demo and we got to compete against draft horses in a log-skidding event. In log-skidding, the human ground-drives the horse, or in our case, donkey, through a course of cones while dragging a log. Teams are timed and a clean run with all cones left standing is necessary. We started through at a trot, curving in and out of the cones with inches to spare. When we made the turn for the finish, I asked for a bit more speed. Ernest gave me a happy little kick-out in the lines and cantered for the finish. It was fun—Ernest was a crowd favorite, but more than that, he liked seeing himself in the company of these draft horse equals. As for me, skidding with the big boys—men in coveralls and flannel shirts and handle-bar mustaches—was a chance to be on the receiving end of the *what-is-this-world-coming-to* look. We came away with a third place ribbon that says "Draft Horse" on it. From our 36" tall vantage point, it was a *huge* win!

For the afternoon performance, we were harnessed, hitched, and ready when the class before us went in. We were parked at the side of a road to the performance arena, when six teams of draft horses, with six horses in each team, passed by us at a high trot. Exhilarating was an understatement: Color! Sound! Drama! The ground shook as one huge team after another thundered past us. Ernest stood with a hip cocked in loose lines, knowing they were just his opening act. We should all have such self-respect.

The Birthday that Changed the World

I have always loved my birthday! For all of the days that celebrated other people and events, this day was all mine. I'd been on the farm for almost two years and had finally caught my breath. A celebration was in order. I had treats planned and friends would probably call. The day started early; the dogs were out, horses were fed, the coffee was hot. At 7a.m., I turned on the television for the news.

That day in September, I saw what everyone else saw; the second plane flying into the World Trade Center. I sank to the sofa trying to comprehend what happened. I'd seen images like that in movies before, but please don't let this be real. I didn't drink my coffee. News reports blared on, the videos played again and again—and I worried. I knew people in New York City and Washington DC.

It was silent on my prairie—no cars driving, no people outside. I missed seeing airplanes in the sky while they were grounded; I missed the reminder that people were around me, even if I didn't talk with them. I was scared for the first time since coming to the farm. I called the dogs to the sofa to hold vigil with me.

To say it was the worst birthday ever would be pathetically self-obsessed. The lion's share of horror and loss happened to others; I prayed for them, wept for all of us, and I felt sorry for myself. It happened on my birthday.

Sometimes I paced and looked out the windows, fearing war and breathing dread. I took naps between news reports and woke up exhausted. I only did what had to be done. A few days later the media reported that psychologists were saying that watching the crash again and again on TV was not a great idea. It seemed obvious in hindsight but by the time the media stopped showing the towers tumble, it was too late for me. By then I was stranded on the sofa, eating out of cans.

The horses stared at the house. I went out and did the chores but I didn't ride. It seemed okay to stay on the sofa—almost patriotic. After two or three days, I took a shower and went to the grocery store. Everyone there seemed stilted. Too quick, nervous about making eye contact with people they didn't know. I hurried home, relieved to turn the news on again.

Days later the planes were cleared to fly and eventually I returned to work, no quicker than anyone else. My work phone hadn't rung in weeks but I started tinkering in my studio. Since closing my gallery, I had contracted with other galleries to sell my work and I had work due for the holidays but I felt bruised and worried. I knew the world had changed but I didn't know what that would mean for my farm.

Now the media were encouraging people not to let this event change us as a country—President Bush suggested we get out and shop. I am sure small businesses across the country were as slow as mine. As the holidays approached that year, we all belligerently pretended we were fine, but I saw photos of all of the orphaned children mourn and knew it was a lie. Other artists I knew reported a huge drop in sales, just like me. The national post-traumatic stress that trickled down told us to keep our money in our pockets.

It wasn't the first time world events impacted my work. During the Iran Hostage Crisis in 1979, the gold market took an unprecedented leap and my gallery inventory sat in limbo for a time. Years later the school shootings at Columbine High School were within a few miles of my gallery and our community was in shock and mourning. My work phone was silent and I wondered how long I could hold steady. After a month, the business began to return and I survived the bump.

But September 11th was more than a bump. Months passed

and my sales were dismal; my income dropped by more than half. My fledgling online sales got more attention but few sales. I checked with all my sources and no one was buying anything. My business phone did not ring for the next full year. Each month I held on, thinking that the next month would improve, but it didn't. It's natural with a small business that clients start to feel like friends. And when they stopped coming by, I tried to not take it personally. Finally I had to let my one-day-a-week office space in Denver go.

My career and my identity were so interwoven that my personality became my work. Or vice versa, it was hard to tell. I was a goldsmith. Surviving the early years took so much push that until that moment, I could never have imagined letting go. For the first time, the idea that I might not die with a forging hammer in my hand secretly entered my mind.

Whatever was going on in the news, whatever people were thinking and feeling about 9-11 and the future, the horses had to eat and it had to happen now. I took odd jobs to supplement my income—a friend needed help in her house-cleaning business, a dog kennel nearby needed help, anything I could find. Instead of driving forcefully ahead in my career and not letting anything stand in my way, for the first time I couldn't even see the way. Moving certainly hadn't resolved my midlife crisis; it was still right there chugging along beside me.

Going from being an artist to cleaning other people's bathrooms was a blow, but at the same time, it provided clarity. I worked a day's labor and came home with a check. It was a clean transaction in a world that seemed increasingly confusing. I was proud to be resourceful and all the while, I told myself that next month work would be different. Some days my most creative accomplishment was finding a way to feed the horses; it was an art form of its own. Still I believed if I held on and just didn't panic, I would get back on track. I said that for the whole next year.

Circumstances lingered. I kept an open mind and took what was offered. My animals didn't miss a meal. When a friend got sick, I helped her. She insisted on paying me. When people found out that I was available to ferry loved ones to the doctor, I got more requests. I had become the person asked to help out, a jill-of-all-trades with a little bit of whatever was needed by whoever asked. I got called away from my goldsmith workbench to be a horse show secretary, a dog-sitter, a landscaper. I never knew where the week would take me—it was chaotic and erratic and busy. Like riding a wave and trusting its direction when the destination wasn't clear.

Nothing changed about my passion for art or horses or my life at the farm, but I had changed; I had to find a way to be more financially creative. The change was so gradual that I didn't notice at first, but my old career began to feel too limited, too closed off from everything. Being a goldsmith was a desk job. The world had been tossed and bounced and when it came to a stop, the career that I loved was in the way of who I wanted to be. I was going on fifty and I had a lot of reinventing to do.

Every few months an old client complained about the disappointing news that I wasn't still sitting at my workbench, waiting for their call.

"Consider it a change of media," I said.

The Best Bad Dog

Her name didn't start out to be Spam. She got demoted to that name. In the beginning she was Lucille, my future ex-husband's dog. Back before they were called Australian Cattle Dogs, they were just called Heelers. The first time I saw a Heeler was in the movie *Road Warrior*. Mel Gibson shared a can of Dinky Do dog food with a gnarly Heeler who was clearly smarter than him or anyone else in the movie, and my fate was sealed that day. I love a good bad-dog. Some dogs have a grating teacher's pet sort of attitude, living to play fetch and wagging entirely too much. I like a more cynical dog.

It was the same year I got Spirit—1987. The ugly truth is that we got Spam from a pet store, the kind that buys from puppy mills. We didn't know it was the worst possible place to get a dog back then, but we learned.

My parents were visiting during one of our breaks from estrangement. It was a pattern—my parents and I couldn't become friends and we couldn't quit each other. My future ex-husband and I were at the mall with them for one of those antique shows that sell cheap reproductions. My parents searched booths for that rare find: an actual antique. Likely, we all just wanted to be out in a larger space than my living room.

I sat on a bench, trying to get rid of a sinus headache. Parental visits always had that effect on me. My mother joined me and asked where my husband was. I nodded toward a pet store; he was inside holding a puppy on his lap, surrounded by little girls. The puppy had a salt-and-pepper coat, a large black spot over one eye, and a docked tail. He had already named her Lucille.

My mother used her practical voice, so well-practiced after years having a daughter prone to stupid decisions. "Oh, don't let him get a dog," she warned. I smiled the usual passive aggressive smile, also well-practiced, and reminded her that I had three dogs at home. "Mom, it would be so hypocritical, coming from me."

Two days later, my parents had gone and we had the puppy at an all-night emergency vet clinic, limp with Giardia and totally dehydrated. There's always a guaranteed trip to the emergency vet with a puppy-mill dog from a mall pet store. My future ex-husband sobbed, pleading with them to save her. I almost didn't recognize him with furrowed eyebrows and squinty eyes. We held hands and worried for her little tiny life. I felt his clammy fingers tense up, straining to hear the vet on the other side of the door. I fell in love with him all over seeing his besotted puppy love. A few hundred dollars later, the puppy came home.

Not that the love was ever returned by the puppy, who would never be a Lucille either. She ignored him totally and kept total eye contact on me, as constant as gravity. She was skanky and foul tempered, as unlikable as a puppy can be. She never wagged a hair. She seemed more like a Spam to me.

The divorce followed in a few months. There was no drama like in the emergency room. The puppy love faded along with everything else and my almost ex-husband and I took our home apart. He didn't want Spam. He said she reminded him of me. I couldn't find an apartment that would let me have my three dogs, much less all four.

We bartered a deal over the lives of my good dogs. He ended up with my two older dogs, Tess and Aggie. They were calm and sweet, and they stayed in their house with him. The young unruly dogs, Spam and Fritz, a rescue Doberman, came with me. Maybe it was for the best, if a divorce had such a thing. I took baby steps loading the moving boxes. The dogs watched me leave as my ex-husband planned his upcoming nuptials. I drove off with half the pack, feeling like a monster. Part of each day from then on, I worried about my separated dogs and wondered how divorced parents with actual children could live with themselves.

The dogs and I moved into one of those marginal apartments in a transitional neighborhood. Spirit was safe at his boarding barn. Fritz kept watch on us and Spam was on the way to becoming a legend. At twelve weeks, she had propelled herself out of my arms, attacking a bewildered golden retriever for the crime of looking at me. She grasped his neck with sharp little puppy teeth and dangled like a bad tie. She had a cocky walk and frequently lifted her leg to pee—once on an elegant friend's imported Italian pumps, previously a butter-soft, hunter green color. Her hind legs were rudely spread too far apart when she sat down, making anyone around uncomfortable about their own knees.

Sometimes guests would ask me what Spam was staring at. From another room, I'd answer, "Is she staring at me through the wall?" They affirmed it looked like she was. She never took her eyes off me.

If you felt the need to bend over and pet her, she shook you off like dirt. And if you scratched her belly, total retaliation was fair response. One day Spam snapped at a blond woman who baby-talked to her. Of course I didn't dream of reprimanding her for that. Baby talk offends me too.

There were only two men Spam ever liked. One was a cowboy who came to the gallery. He had a swagger just like hers but when he playfully tried to get her to leave with him once, he wasn't able to drag all thirty-five pounds of her to the door. The other man she loved was a photographer from New York. He was thin with hunched-over narrow shoulders, rancid black hair and pasty white skin. He was a constant smoker and she just adored him. Like me, there was no accounting for her taste in men.

Spam came to work with me each day at the gallery. It's possible that some people came to see her instead of me. Spam was a rare breed then, but more than that she was an enigma, she had a body language of toughness and intelligence. Or maybe an artistic temperament, which was my excuse. She was proof that fawning over people isn't as interesting as almost anything else. When I saw commercials on TV about people looking like their pets, I wasn't entirely comfortable.

At the same time, I couldn't take my eyes off her either. It was like seeing myself in a dog costume, or through someone else's eyes. Her contrary ways had a way of attracting people. People she growled at in her sullen way smiled back and cooed to her, albeit from a safe distance. Above all, her confidence was electric. Neither of us felt like we fit in and it made us abrasive. But she was cool about it.

Spam held a bad opinion about vets since getting spayed. She developed a violent infection that took two more surgeries to repair. After that Spam had enough vets for a life-time. That vet claimed, from what she could tell, Spam's parents were most likely siblings. Maybe that was a key to her unique temperament. And another reason to avoid pet stores in malls.

When Spam was five, she developed an increasingly foul-smelling stench in her mouth that didn't go away. It wasn't a dog breath, this smelled more like rotten meat. A vet visit was required, but getting her inside a vet office would be a major undertaking. I resolved that whole ordeal by calling a mobile vet to the gallery. I warned the vet about Spam and she arrived in jeans and a shirt, looking like most of my clients. Spam recognized her occupation immediately with a low growl. I sat on a chair with Spam in my lap.

"Can you see it?" I said, as I carefully lifted Spam's lips apart while the vet peered from a distance. Spam continued the long growl note without taking a breath. It wasn't clear, but the vet guessed it was probably an infected tooth.

When we arrived at the clinic for surgery, I knew I'd probably hold her for the first shot. The vet tech began gagging almost immediately—Spam smelled a little worse by the hour. I volunteered to assist the vet during the surgery. Spam wouldn't have let anyone else touch her anyway. I got her on the operating table using a wrestling move I had learned from a high-school boyfriend, and the vet started the anesthesia. Once the vet felt safe, she opened Spam's mouth to find a really nasty melanoma that looked like black mold. The teeth were all fine. She took out as much of the cancer as she could and then prepared a sample to send off to the lab, along with some x-rays. The vet and I talked about hard options and sat with Spam as she was waking up—she forgot to growl in her hung-over state.

Spam and I met with oncology specialists a few days later. They surrounded us tall, expert, and unlikeable. Their recommendation was removing half her jaw. She would still be able to eat soft food and probably drool a lot. They gave her two months to live without the surgery. We went home to ponder the decision.

The next morning Spam and I met a friend at the gallery before business hours. I needed to talk it out; I didn't trust the specialists and I didn't want to lose her. Spam sprawled out by my feet in a shaft of morning sun from the open door, passively disinterested in our chatter. Suddenly, a German shepherd dog on one of those silly retractable leashes burst onto the entry step of the gallery. There was a tug on that small cord to the shepherd's collar, but in an instant, Spam flew, hit him body to body, and knocked him back six feet. She pinned the male shepherd to the sidewalk, while the shepherd's owner barked anger at all of us. Spam weighed less than half what the bigger dog weighed, but was on top with her teeth around the large dog's neck.

My turn to bolt out the door. Spam came to my side as I used my contrite voice. "Is your dog all right? Should we take him to the vet and get him checked?"

I apologized profusely, the shepherd cowered, more afraid of his owner than Spam, while his owner tried to act like his ego was intact. Somewhere in this dogfight, my decision was made. It was counterintuitive; Spam was always a challenge, she was dog-aggressive. I didn't ever want her to fight. At the same time, taking half her jaw would disable her too much in her life. No surgery. She couldn't do without her jaw.

I did take Spam to an acupuncturist I was seeing. It wasn't my intention but when I called to cancel my ongoing appointments, in favor of paying Spam's vet bills, the doctor invited Spam. During these gratis visits, Spam got poked with needles and told she was beautiful. I cowered, remembering the baby-talking blond, but Spam apparently liked acupuncturists much more than blonds or vets. Two months passed and Spam didn't die. Maybe it was the acupuncture or maybe Spam's constitution was just too toxic for cancer to survive.

Spam thrived another decade, to grouse and pout and stare at me. She led the pack without a smile. When she was beside me, one of her front paws always rested on top of my foot as a constant reminder of who was in charge. Spam did not cuddle and she did not play. We co-habited with a steely unspoken connection. We understood each other. Her love was fierce.

Spam was thirteen when we moved to the farm, a good age for a dog to slow down some and think about retirement. Not Spam though, she didn't let up. At the same time, she recognized the farm like it was her long lost childhood home. There was an exhale from her soul, a slightly less cantankerous peace in her. When the neighbor's cows came too close to the fence, she moved a few yards onto their land, to stand guard staring the cows down and keeping us safe. Although Spam had free run of the farm, mostly she stayed a few feet away from me, like my own Secret Service agent. When I rode a horse, she trotted behind. If we had been out on a trail it might have made sense, but dressage horses work in an arena and do a fair number of circles. It was hard work following in sand footing but she panted along until I put her into a down stay in the middle of the arena so she could rest. Each ride went this way, and it might have been good exercise for Hero, the young dog, but Spam was stiff with arthritis and fairly blind. She was probably deaf or at least she acted that way when it suited her.

She was the kind of old dog you could only stand to live with if you remembered her young, and then just barely. We had gone down a long road together, complicated and intense. Friends always thought she was a rescue dog that never settled in, never quite called a place home. I knew the feeling. After a few months, Spam began to lie in the shade of the barn and glare at my ride from there. The view was good for relentless watching and sometimes she let herself sleep. There were moments that she seemed almost satisfied. Those were golden days.

The next year, when Spam was fourteen, she began to have seizures. Every few weeks I found her looking off in the distance, disoriented. In a few moments she would return to herself. Then she had five big seizures in two days and she couldn't walk or stand. I spent a day lying on the floor next to her, telling her stories of her greatest triumphs and reminding her what a legend she was. I cooked her chicken that she didn't eat. Her foggy old eyes were very quiet.

My vet and I talked at length. It was late afternoon by then and Spam wasn't in pain. Some dogs come out of it, the vet said, and we set a time to bring her in the next morning. Spam didn't eat, but she did manage to growl at me when I moved her to her usual spot on the floor beside the bed. Sometimes a complaint is as good as a kiss from a cranky old dog. She never did sleep on the bed and that night was no different.

We woke up early to a bright clean day, but there was no improvement. Spam couldn't balance enough to stand, she was dull eyed and seemed constantly disoriented. With all the courage I could muster, I declared her to be a very good bad dog, the very best, and carefully carried her to the front porch. I thought she might like to watch the sun rise while I did chores.

I quietly cried into the horse's manes as I fed and watered, trying to purge as much sadness as I could. Spam wasn't big on tears and I wanted to spare her mine. I thought I'd bury her when we got back. First I had a hole to dig. So I took the shovel and walked to the area I thought to use, passing her on the front porch on my way. Spam was in the position I had left her and I spoke some words meant to comfort her.

Spam lifted her head and looked directly at me. Response! She stood up and shook her tough little body. She came down the steps onto the driveway and walked past me to a flower-bed where she lifted her leg and peed. Then she said, in a voice clear and strong, "I am not dead yet, you can put the shovel away."

I knew a hug was out of the question, so I obediently put the shovel away and made her breakfast. She and I had battled for dominance each day of our fifteen years, and I was well aware that I might win a battle now and then, but never the war. That was just the way I wanted it. I like bad dogs. Old bad dogs are even sweeter. She won the day, and I was glad to yield.

A few days later, we had an appointment to get more meds from the vet. She woke up slowly that morning, and after breakfast, she gave me a look somewhere between confusion and surrender. Her energy was softer and her lack of temper apparent. As the morning went on, she was a tiny bit clingy, and I knew something was different today. She never wanted to be this close.

When it was time to go, she let me lift her into the truck without making a complaint. Once I was settled, she scooted across the bench seat, and laid her head on my lap. Lots of dogs do this as a matter of course but Spam always sat as far away as possible. I felt the weight of her flat little head on my thigh, her ears just a little too far apart, with bittersweet calm. I put my hand on her back and she let it stay there the whole way.

Spam stayed through the hard part of this midlife crisis. She was my last dog to know my parents. She was with me when they passed. We had family history that was different from the dogs who came later. She kept me strong until we found our home farm.

They say the great loves in our lives change us. I have never been so possessed by a dog, but it was a dark hold, bound up in vulnerability and control. I understand complicated love a bit more now. Independence and inter-dependence is always a question for strong-minded dogs and hard-headed women. It was a prickly place that we shared. We both grew some compassion and tolerance because of our acceptance of each other. Okay, maybe one of us more than the other, but then, one of us needed it more.

Being Jane Goodall

My high-school horse-friend went to Stanford University in the mid-1970's and she had the opportunity to travel to Africa to study wild chimpanzees with Jane Goodall. In the jungle! Her trip changed *my* life. I'd been watching animals and reading body language since long before I knew the words for it, but this was the first time I'd heard it labeled scientific research. Goodall's work in the jungle was widely respected, not just a young girl's pastime.

What if Jane Goodall and I walked the same path?

Dreams were not encouraged in our home but if I had one, it was to get far away, to soften the constant flinch in my gut, to let the anxiety drain. Animals had been our livelihood on our farm and my father drew hard lines between them and us. Cute babies were farm assets and my father believed there was no place for a soft heart in the farming business. Every animal had a job and if it wasn't earning its way, it was dispensable. It's impossible to romanticize the old farm even now. My farm would be different.

Dr. Leakey gave Jane Goodall the research job in Gombe, Africa, partly because he thought she had the temperament to handle isolation for long periods of time.

On my farm, the dogs were the only ones immediately thrilled with its stinky pond and large bunny population. It was an immediate improvement for them, but the rest of us—lame horses, frightened cats and overwhelmed human—were trying to find our footing. This life was not full of compliments and cash like my gallery had been. There were fewer distractions on the prairie and my own species was rare. The weather was no longer small talk, instead it directed my day. My desire to go past the end of the driveway was non-existent. I had the temperament.

Sometimes I wondered if I was living Jane's life in microcosm; in a five-acre farm in Colorado sort of way. Did she have days of doubt in the jungle at first? Did she think she had stepped off a cliff not knowing where she would land?

By the time the immediate work of settling the move slowed down, the farm got very quiet. I had been running/proving/surviving from house to house, relationship to relationship, day to day for years and then all that noise stopped. The stillness of the prairie gave me enough space to slow down, neutralizing busy thoughts with solitude. Nature spoke up. I thought I'd always been good at understanding animals but it had been superficial compared to this. My senses blended together to form a dimensional awareness that was more perceptive. As I mimicked the communication I saw in the barn, they taught me more and understanding followed. My body language became fluent, wordless communication.

It was as though my own intellect dulled my senses. I hardly scratched the surface of the awareness necessary for an animal to survive, especially a prey animal. When a horse or dog noticed something that my senses didn't pick up, I tended to label them distracted or spooky. I held them to my low standards of perception. Changing that habit started slowly. Instead of punishing a dog who barked at night, I thanked them for the awareness and wasn't mad if the intruder they warned me about was a squirrel and not a mass murderer. It's the human curse of putting intellect above instinct. I was turning that around.

Jane Goodall was very unusual for her time—she followed the chimps in their habitat instead of a laboratory and slowly became part of the group. She let it get personal, she respected them and gave them names instead of numbers.

My farm was not nearly as exotic as Jane's jungle, but there was research to be done and so I watched. It's hard to quantify results with cats. Especially if they know you're watching. Hank, the barn cat, did chores with me and each morning laid out a couple of mouse corpses before I got a scoop of grain fed to each of the horses, as if hunting was a timed event. He saw himself as a big cat—zoo big—and he enjoyed being a bully. Hank made dogs twice his size cower and whimper like babies.

I tried watching Spam and Hero. Being cattle dogs, they always positioned themselves on my heels, so they were hard to observe. Mainly they watched me staring at them. It was a standoff. Llama research was as peaceful and sweet until an intruder came. Then it was all spit and toenails to protect us. Goat research always gave mixed data and involved some level of destruction: How did that goat get inside the truck?

But I was never really an equal opportunity researcher. Horses were my priority. My eyes always returned to Spirit and Dodger. They had a rhythm in all things from chewing to galloping. While they were boarded at another barn, I saw only an abbreviated part of their lives, but now they told me about rest and play, the peace of moving together as a herd. I and the other members of our herd all acknowledged them as the elite animals of the farm and they ruled with peace and kindness.

Since before horses were first immortalized in cave paintings down through time until today, humans have been in awe of their beauty and power. Horses are strong and vulnerable at the same time, and I wanted to emulate that in my world. Living with horses and riding them is a journey of perception and response. It's doing self-therapy astride a thousand-pound sentient animal, with emotions, opinions, and a willingness to negotiate. My father was right that animals should have some respect for humans. I just wanted a different kind of leadership, and I studied the herd to see how they did it.

Jane didn't have a formal scientific education, or even a general college degree, just like me. Photos showed Jane sitting with a notebook, watching. She must have used curiosity and intuition as tools.

While I worked outside, the animals stayed close. As I mucked out the pens, each in turn would come to greet me. The horses usually positioned themselves between me and the muck cart so I had to stop. We exchanged breath and then they usually showed me a place that was itchy and I obliged. We might move each other's feet a bit. It's what herding dogs and cutting horses know; a kind of two-step dance of following each other's steps. Sometimes they started it, sometimes me. The more I didn't push, the more they offered.

Cues to move away from the muck cart were as small as a point of my finger, as effortless as an exhale. Everyone came running when I called them by name—it always meant something good. There is a special sweetness when a horse offers his eye, when they follow your feet without a lead rope. Body language is universal and more expressive than words, but you have to stop talking to hear it. It's as easy as catching a cat. You just stop chasing.

In an immense jungle, Jane must have seen a natural law unfold in all their shared lives, something like what I call the circle of life. It's neither good or bad, and at the most, impersonal. The design of nature is perfect if you sit back and watch a while.

The line between the domesticated animals on my farm and wild animals was only as wide as a smooth wire fence. Ducks on the pond talked to the ducks that provided my eggs. I got familiar with the nice coyote couple who lived on the far side of the pond. Half-Tail was as big as a German shepherd dog and his mate was softly confident and more relaxed in her body than most coyotes; she never skulked about. Each spring when whelping time was close, she laid in the sun belly up and glowing.

The coyotes would chat with my dogs under the stars and then after a few quiet weeks, I heard the high-pitched yodels and squeals of her pups discovering the night sky. She and Half-Tail taught them to hunt ducklings on the pond. They took a stealth approach and then had a water fight. The pups would pounce and the ducklings would skitter across the water like skipping stones. They managed to thin out the ducklings, but whether they caught them or drowned them in the commotion, was impossible to tell. It wasn't about win or lose, just the circle of life rolling along. I never contradicted the law, but sometimes I asked the coyotes to go away if I had company coming. A flotilla of ducklings is endearing to see and I knew that the inevitable was only postponed for a few hours.

Jane learned that the chimps had a complex social system, with patterns of recognizable behavior, including discernible communication methods.

The herd provided an early warning system on the farm. I had a hearing loss from too many untreated ear infections as a kid, so I had to pay attention; I had to make the effort to *try* to hear. It took less effort here, since I had a whole herd who sounded off a warning for guests of any species. Starting with a donkey bray loud enough to overcome deafness, followed by some barking. Locating the intruder in the field behind us was a simple triangulation of llama nose directions—they are very curious. It was the llamas who introduced me to Half-Tail and his mate for the first time. The UPS man got stopped at the front gate by a few llamas who wanted to smell his breath. They stretched forward over the gate, noses at the ready. I don't know what he was afraid of. They don't even have upper teeth but it was enough to make him slip my delivery quickly over and hurry back to the truck.

The same early warning system worked for weather forecasting and health issues. Subtle changes in horse behavior told me when the barometer was changing and a front was on the way. If the llamas and donkey were in the barn early, weather was close and there would probably be lightning as well. It gave me time to get the horses in from the pasture.

Other times there was a different kind of change in the air, and I could follow it to the animal who needed help. They trusted me to doctor them; I gave shots and bandaged like a pro, but if it was too much, finding the animal sooner meant I could call the vet sooner.

Domestic animals are not immune to the circle of life, but there was some wiggle room. An elderly or lame horse won't survive long in the wild, but domestic horses had stall rest to recuperate safely and the elders could be given extra help and protection. There were remedies for pain and infection. Arthritis could be managed.

My father would have disowned me again for this foolish waste of money. Animals who outlived their usefulness should be killed. On his farm, survival depended on income over expense, man controlling nature for his benefit. Now on my farm I invested in retirement and uselessness, because benefiting animals in the gray area between the laws of nature and domestic life was rewarding.

Jane Goodall wrote that each chimp had a personality, that their lives were filled with drama, comedy, and tragedy. Her greatest discovery was that the chimps made tools and ate meat, meaning people had to look at chimps with a different eye. Chimpanzees were more like us humans than previously thought.

My farm family lived. That's all—they just expressed their lives and their personalities. Rudeness was noted, friendships grew. The benevolent older leaders watched out for the youngest and weakest. The goat who believed he was a llama had absolutely no sense of humor about it. The llamas begged to be cooled off in the heat of the day, loving the civilized convenience of a garden hose. The ducks were pagans. The cats were murder-at-large for small creatures. The dogs worked the hardest, like corporate over-achievers who never took a day off. But the horses ruled, with grace and intelligence and the most whole-hearted connection to something greater—they took us all to church.

And then there were the donkeys, the moral compass of any farm. Donkeys showed kindness to everyone—they had a confidently evolved sense of manner and fairness. A human had to be worthy of their trust; it wasn't given lightly. But with trust, miracles were possible.

They were all my teachers and my family. They encouraged me to be as honest as they were and we learned to work together. Lots of trainers use intimidation and dominance thinking it gets quicker results, but it is never the animal's best work if fear is the motivator. And fear, after all, is what I ran to the barn to escape in the first place, all those years ago.

My earliest language was reading the visual signs: the dog wagging his tail or the stomp-bang of my father's boot. The first months on my farm were like an immersion language course and I had no option but to get more fluent. I read their bodies and facial expressions and answered with mine, and the animals came running: feral cats, dogs that hated everybody, and horses that no one could catch. The more I mimicked and more I asked politely, the more the animals volunteered. Rudeness on either side was corrected and forgotten. Breathing was our common ground. Conversations continued for hours in a place between empathy and intuition. They all communicated in the usual way, it was me that changed. I evolved. After so many years of patience from generations of animals, I finally remembered a universal language that I had known in the beginning. Living in a human world had dumbed me down and I lost trust with words: verbal conversations had double messages—some were passive-aggressive, some just plain dishonest.

If the study of animals gave real researchers like Ms. Goodall more knowledge about humans as a species, then I concur. We are more alike than we are different. My greatest discovery? The animals all *wanted* to get along. They made our multi-species farm a peaceable kingdom. I forgot to be lonely. I got used to conversation in the quiet. They reminded me daily that acceptance and acknowledgment is really all any of us want. Somewhere in the process I stopped just being a human who liked animals. I switched teams entirely. *Did Jane do that?*

Dogs to the Rescue

Some rescue dogs land in a new home like they were re-born that day with no history to hold them back. But most are a bit like Fritz. He was a young Doberman with an eye swollen shut and a big cut on his head that looked infected. In the early 1980's in Denver, I worked with a teen runaway hotline, and ended up counseling a young girl who was abused and lost. She and Fritz were skinny and dirty from living in alleys and eating out of dumpsters. Now they had to split up. He needed vet care and she was entering a group home. We all knew, even as weak as he was, that this dog had been doing his best for his girl and she was trying to return the favor.

I found a vet who would take a look at Fritz at no charge to our non-profit. He got stitches and some antibiotics. No one at our office could take him home, and he deserved a chance. It was up to me, so I announced loudly that I didn't like Dobermans or women who owned them, and then we left together.

The first morning he was with me, I woke up to him standing at the side of my bed with his long pointy nose two inches from mine. His dark eyes stared into mine and his cropped ears were at attention. I closed my eyes and held my breath, trying to remember what to do when you think a dog is going to attack. Our heads were at the same level. Would he see me as prey? When my eyes finally opened the rest of the way, he exhaled and sat down. I don't know how long he'd been watching me, but from that moment on, he shadowed me, heeling by my side or sitting with his back to mine, watching. Fritz acted like something bad lurked close by. It was something that a lab or golden retriever would never believe, but Fritz must have seen it. He stayed vigilant and waited for the inevitable.

My dogmatic Doberman opinions crumbled the first time he curled up into a tiny ball on the sofa next to me, not wanting to take up any more room than he thought he deserved. Fritz gobbled each meal, certain there would never be more. He cowered around children, as if they were agents of the devil. The sight of an electric cord set him off quivering, like it was the most frightening weapon of all. I never changed his mind so I fed him slowly and put him in the yard when it was time to vacuum. I protected him.

He came to work with me for years and spent the day sleeping with my other dogs in back. Every so often, someone came into the gallery who didn't seem quite right to me. I called Fritz and he'd wander out from the back room with sleepy eyes to sit by me. I banked on the stranger making the common assessment: If he was trained to sit, he was probably trained to attack as well. If the stranger had good intentions, he would compliment Fritz; if not he would leave quickly. Fritz was a timid dog who was nervous about most everything but he wore a Doberman suit, a real life sheep in wolf's clothing.

The vet explained to me that this breed was prone to bad heart issues, and he would probably not live a long life. So we began navigating our shared time with caution and low expectations. Through all the years that Fritz was with me, he never forgot his beginnings. He never felt safe, and trust was always hard for him. Just like me.

During the holidays, when I felt the most at odds with my own species, Fritz and I shared popcorn and movies—and the knowledge that there was evil in the world. We had seen it in our families. We looked strong and tough on the outside, but we were hanging on by a thread most days. Each of us, still rescue animals, still trying to find our way home.

As he got old, his eye sight was bad and sometimes he would

snap at me, and then be horrified as soon as his vision cleared. Fritz had developed a sort of dementia. He forgot to be afraid; cords no longer made him cringe. He spent long summer days sleeping in the grass, his bony old body soft and sun-warm. Fritz never demanded my attention. He was just grateful to be there. He became incontinent, but the dementia was such a blessing, that I just bought a bunch of washable rubber-backed rugs.

We met on the sofa every night at nine. He was too old to walk anymore, so Fritz curled up close and had a peace-nap while I watched TV and let my brain slow down. I did it for him, but that hour became the anchor of my day. In those days I hurried so much that life became two dimensional, but on the sofa, stress gave way to gratitude.

There is a magic transformation that happens with good old dogs; one day at a time, they become greater than their body, softer and lighter. And if we have loved them long and well, any challenge at the end is near feels like a gift. Each day is precious. Dogs teach us forgiveness because they demonstrate it. The other word for it is rescue.

Fritz passed a few months before we moved to the farm. He slowly became a walking skeleton. He stayed with us for almost seventeen years and in the end, I think he had a paw in introducing us to our next puppy, too.

Puppy breath is one of those addictive smells that isn't actually pleasing aromatically. Still, who doesn't inch their nose dangerously close to those tiny teeth, just for a whiff of puppy breath?

Just a couple of weeks after Fritz passed, on a bright Sunday morning while driving to the barn to ride, I saw a sign on a ranch gate: "Heeler Pups." This is where Fritz came in, I think he might have turned the wheel. But there I was, looking at a litter of vampire Cattle Dog puppies—all pointy little ears and razor teeth! There was torn-up newspaper and a scattering of left-over puppy chow. The pups were wrestling and yipping in a puppy version of a barroom brawl. A pale-colored one was sitting quietly to the side, staring me right in the eye.

"Hello. I think you're looking for me," he said. He acted like he recognized me or had been expecting me. It was personal. I shook my head and went to ride.

Four hours later, on the way back from the barn, my truck turned into the ranch driveway again. Some of the pups were gone, but the pale one was still in the same spot, with the same quiet eye contact. He looked like a young James Dean. I took a big whiff. His breath was exquisite. We each made a choice and never looked back. We drove home without a whimper. If he noticed his siblings weren't with us, he didn't care.

You almost have to feel sorry for a pup who came into a home with me and Spam. It was just after my mom died, I was pretty depressed, and Spam was dog-aggressive. It was about half-time in my midlife crisis, just months before my move and I felt heart-sore and wounded much of the time. I named him Hero. It was a big name for a little pup, but that was what I needed.

Introducing a puppy to Spam was a prickly guess. She was opinionated and cranky and aggressive. I knew she would have a run at him, but pups don't respond the same way a grown dog would. Still there was no way to know what she would do with a puppy. Or to a puppy. I mostly didn't think she would actually kill Hero. Probably not.

I came up with an introduction plan on the way home. I carried Hero around the side of the house to the back yard and put him down. He made no whimper, just looked at me with passive, Buddha eyes. Then I went across the patio to the back door, called Spam out, and stood back. I knew it would be worse if I held him.

She saw him and bolted toward him, fast and hard. In a less time than a gasp, she was on top of him, pinning him down with her jaws. None of us made a sound. No one moved. I held my breath, frightened for all of us. Had she snapped his puppy neck?

After a long pause, she lifted her head. He hadn't flinched

or tried to escape. He may have played dead but he was so submissive that Spam's teeth relaxed and her stare gripped him instead. He stood up and shook his head and walked further into the yard. Spam pressed her nose against his rump and followed. And followed some more. For two solid hours, Hero marched around in circles in the yard with Spam's nose in full contact, herding Hero along. Sometimes she pushed. Little Hero was covered with spit. Drenched and spiked, even his ears were wet. He looked like a hair product disaster. When he could be pushed not one step farther, he collapsed. His nose hit the ground first and the rest of his body dropped on top of his feet. And he slowly rolled onto his side. He was sticky and gaunt and flat. Maybe she'd killed him after all.

Spam stared at him for a while longer but he didn't have the strength to open his eyes. She went a few strides away and lay down with a satisfied moan and I dropped into a chair in exhausted relief. It was like being jumped into a gang. It was a baptism by spit. Hero was now family.

Each time I get a new dog, I try a different training approach. With Hero I decided that any time he asked me for my attention, I would give it to him. It sounds simple, like an expanded version of the sofa time with Fritz. It meant being open to hear him constantly.

Kids were always in the way in my family, better seen and not heard. Instead of saying "Not now, I'm busy," and making a mental note to cuddle Hero later, I stopped what I was doing and took time to acknowledge him each time he asked. It didn't require much discipline from him, but took a whole lot on my part because I was so busy and important. Each time Hero came to me, I bent down and scratched him and mumbled a few words. Then he would be on his way and I would be left feeling warm and thoughtful. Almost like the plan was that he acknowledged me, allowing me to settle when I needed it, instead of vice versa.

Everything changed when I slowed down. I had always been

the one who spent more time with animals than anyone else but I did it in a hurry. So now I taught myself to be slower—whether it was on the sofa with Fritz or stopping on the way to wash dishes to scratch Hero. I took the time. The animals aren't any different than they ever were. Still, once I stopped speeding, the scope of each of our personalities expanded.

Hero grew up in Spam's shadow. We all did; there was room enough. Hero was silent for so many years that I thought he was mute. He didn't make a peep of any kind until two full years after Spam passed on. Once Hero was sure it was safe and she was really truly gone, he started chattering away and never shut up. He used growls when he was happy and moaned long winded songs that he almost had the words for when he was alone in another room. He just liked the sound of his own voice. At some point he started hugging. Anyone he could grab, he leaned in close and wrapped his front legs around them and then held on. Just a little too long. Like your elderly aunt, pinching painfully tight, but with the kindest intentions. Hero's natural personality was a hundred times better than anyone I could have trained him to be. I was right to shut up and listen.

Die Hard on the Prairie

Chatting about the weather passes the time. It's the subject at the center of the small-talk universe. "How about this heat?" Strangers have common ground; it's something to say in grocery stores and parking lots right after hello. Living in a city and talking about the weather is the tiniest of small talk because the population is a bit removed from the environment, like a bio-dome compared to my new high-desert reality. Lawns get watered into greenhouse perfection in town and the heat of lives and businesses change the air. Even the buildings do double duty as wind fences. In really bad weather, it's a more temperate place and your neighbors are there with you. Sometimes the city has a snow day and roads close, kids get a day out of school, and everyone has a little more to talk about than usual. In all my years in Denver, I didn't know I was living in a bio-dome. I didn't drive out of town in bad weather, how could I know?

Talk of weather in a rural feed store is just as common, but more depends on it. The term *wind chill* is not ever small talk. You can never say the weather is a surprise on the prairie, because everything is visible approaching from the crest of the horizon. It's just that I was amazed at the powerful impact of the weather. The weather educated me in ways I didn't expect and there was no back talk allowed. Winter has the blandest of colors: tan, khaki, beige, and taupe. They've been singing songs about the prairie wind since pioneer days because when the biggest obstacle to slow it down is a fence post, the wind has absolute freedom. Resistance is futile. The first year on the farm, I took enough trips to the south fence line to retrieve my lawn chairs and feed buckets to learn that all decisions must be made with wind direction in mind. I thought those judgments ended at the back door, but even that was premature. I chose the northwest corner of the house for my studio because it gave me the best view of the barn. It was also the wind-ravaged corner. That room was so cold the first winter that I put plastic on the inside of the windows. It blew off.

That winter on the farm forced some adjustment. My salon-boy show horses toughened up quicker than I did. They grew thick winter coats and shared piles of extra hay. By now they had taken a liking to this rural life. Moving them to the farm was a choice to let them live in a more natural way, but that doesn't mean I enjoyed seeing nature smeared all over their bodies. My show horses lay in manure and took turns rolling in a sandy hole in the pasture. I let them be horses but it hurt my eyes just a bit to see them scruffy and unkempt. Does that sound superficial? Having the horses looking well-groomed was my way of letting them and everyone else know what they meant to me. It wasn't cosmetic, it was commitment.

My three-sided barn was built at just the right angle to block the wind. Horses will tolerate almost any other weather condition better than the wind. It must over-stimulate all their senses. Maybe their skin follicles get agitated or maybe the ambient smells go wild, but they get as unsettled as the environment. It didn't help seeing objects flying through the air, either. I began to see that living here had its own particular set of natural stresses for them, different than being in a stall in a closed barn. I guarded their safety with the knowledge that there were no other eyes on them. There was no one else to catch my mistakes.

Some days the temperature could drop by forty degrees and the unsettled weather contributed to the possibility of colic. Horses have a fragile digestive system and colic is the number one cause of equine fatality. It is an ugly painful death if not treated quickly. Owning horses at home meant vigilantly watching for everything that could go wrong night or day. My stress level joined theirs in bad weather. None of us rested well that first winter. Water hoses froze, tank heaters worked overtime. The muck froze so hard to the ground that it stayed there till spring. If the ground was not frozen and slick, it was muddy and slick. Sometimes they shivered and although I knew that was nature's way of finding warmth, it caused me a nearly intolerable pain. I fed them more hay and shivered along with them.

Last thing every night, I bundled up and went out for the late barn check. I heard the nickering as soon as I left the house. Dodger had a high pitched nicker that a horse with less confidence would have kept to himself. Spirit had a deep, slow Barry White sort of nicker. The goats mumbled through their cud, the llamas watched from their group cush. Spirit and Dodger nuzzled their gratitude with warm breath and soft eyes as I threw overnight hay into the pen. Then one last body check for clean legs, soft eyes and fresh manure, and time for me to tuck in, too. The barn held us all together. Whatever problems didn't get resolved during the day, got turnout for the night.

Heading into the second winter I felt better prepared. I was hitting my stride somewhat and we'd been through all the seasons once. I knew it wasn't windy or cold forever. The art of waiting out weather was tolerable as long as I was stocked up on groceries for everybody. By the time February came and the sun started to be warm again, it happened. It was the storm that didn't follow the rules. It started on an ordinary afternoon. The wind blew extra hard and dark clouds ran fast to the south. Soon the snow started and by the time I bundled up to do the midnight feeding, the snow was a few inches deep. Everyone looked fine, tucked in with hay, and spring was on the way. No big deal.

The next morning the sun just didn't come up. I checked the clock twice. By the time it was finally light out, the wind was blowing so hard that I couldn't see the barn. I couldn't even see the pen attached to the barn and that wasn't fifty feet from my window. The snow was as dense as fog. Horses need a minimum of five gallons of water a day. Would the horses come out to the edge where the water tank was in this weather? I could see snow everywhere but there was no way to tell how much was on the ground. It was a solid wall with no visibility at all.

I put a stiff pair of Carhartt coveralls on, with a jacket on top, two hats and a muffler tied around that, and finally, layered gloves. When I got outside the back door the wind was so intense that I couldn't open my eyes. This was how people got disoriented. I put a hand out and then shuffled one blind foot in front of the other with my head tucked down. I followed the wall of the porch to the back-yard fence, then hand over hand to the gate. Through the gate I had to go straight to hit the paddock fence but I had nothing to guide me. It was like stepping into the void. What if I missed the barn and got turned around? What if I fell and couldn't get up again in the wind? I couldn't open my eyes, my face stung like needles and I groped my hands out in front of me and counted baby steps through the snow. It took forever. Did I miss the paddock?

At the farm on Leaf River we had winters this brutal and people died of exposure. I could remember tunneling out of the house with snow above the windows. That weighed on my mind; if I died taking care of the animals, who would take care of the animals? Is this when people panic? I couldn't tell which way the wind was blowing. It seemed to be coming at me from all directions at once.

Finally my hands hit the paddock fence and I grabbed hard, letting it take some of the pressure off my legs. I pulled hand over hand slowly along the fence until I was at the barn door. The two horses and Ernest were in this barn. The snow was up past the horse's fetlocks and their blankets were damp but not wet. Ernest was especially ready for breakfast. I threw extra hay and braced myself for a trip to the water tank. I filled a bucket there and hand over hand, dragged the bucket up inside the barn. I gave each one some grain to up their body temp a bit. I was not so worried about the llamas in the little barn to the west. I'd thrown extra hay last night and they are hearty mountain animals to begin with. The goats were in that barn, too. I'd get inside the house and try to get feeling back in my fingers before checking on them.

It was the same path back, holding the fence panel. The wind felt just as strong this direction, still in my face. I couldn't see even a shadow of the house when I let go of the fence panel and counted steps back toward where I thought the yard was. No gate. No fence. Was this how it happened? But then the fence bumped me and I got back to the porch. The skin of my face was thick and hard from the cold, not that any of it was exposed. I peeled off layers of clothes. Then more layers. I gasped for air, apparently I wasn't breathing out there. Tea would be good.

That was when I noticed the power was out. Well, understandable in this wind. Wind speeds of twenty or twenty-five miles an hour are common enough. But this wind was twice that speed sustained with outlandish gusts that rattled walls. Real wind. Wind that worried barns and trees, and had probably taken out a few local power lines. I hunkered down to think of my resources. No kitchen stove, no camp stove, no gas grill. No hot anything. That meant the fridge was off, so I put some groceries on the front porch. After some cereal I curled in a blanket. It was just past nine in the morning and I was exhausted. The cats and dogs were especially friendly, as the internal temp in the house was down to fifty-four degrees. I decided to let it snow.

When I woke up the view out the window hadn't changed a bit, still zero visibility. Feeding extra hay is about the best help for a horse in a blizzard. Calories keep them warm, so I layered-up and counted steps, visualized fence lines, and got to the barn. The ground blizzard looked like a wall of snow, but once I was outside I could tell that the wind had changed direction. Instead of my barn blocking the wind, it was now catching snow like a baseball mitt. The snow inside the barn was three feet deep; the horses were wet and shivering. The little donkey was shoulder deep and his belly had to be cold.

Throwing hay was the easy part. I pulled the wet blankets off the horses and put wool coolers on, hoping that somehow the horses would dry. Coolers don't have all the buckles a horse blanket has, so they flapped wildly in the wind and made everyone nervous. I trudged back to the trunk and got summer sheets to tie down the coolers.

It was impossible to tell if the horses were drinking enough. I broke the ice out of the water buckets, and followed the fence for more water. The horses couldn't get there now if they wanted to. This time getting through the drifts was much harder and I put my shovel to work. Part of one of the buckets spilled into my boot while dragging the buckets back, introducing me to a whole new level of cold. I really needed a better plan. This storm was spanking all of us. How could I be so badly prepared? The wind hadn't slowed a bit but energy was lagging in all of us—especially Ernest.

My horse blankets were heavy, thick canvas, big enough to cover a bed and soaking wet. I managed to tie straps so I could get both of them secured over my shoulder for dragging and again traced the path back to the house. Blankets made for even slower going, but at the same time there was less chance of me being blown away by a monster gust. The idea of drying the blankets was a good one, but the temperature in the house was dropping so drying became a long-term goal. Why did I even drag them in? The power was still out. No reason to panic. Mainly because panic is a luxury and I was all out of luxury.

When my hands were warm and my feet dry, I headed out again for the little barn. Through the wall of snow, hand over hand and step by step along a different fence, I managed to get to the llamas and goats. The gap between the two barns had created a wind tunnel and the drift was taller than the fence panel. It curved around the shed effectively closing them all inside but leaving a long, skinny triangle on the west side. I could barely wedge myself close enough to peer in. There they were, dry and cheerfully chewing cud. The goats gave me an amiable *naaah-hhh* and there was still hay. There was no way I could get water in for them but they were cousins in the camel family, so their need for water wasn't as extreme as the horses. How long could they hold up in there? When would it end? It was not time to worry now; I needed concentration to find my way back to the house. The tracks I just made had already filled in.

I nibbled a peanut butter sandwich and frowned. Nothing in my house could help. The dogs went out the front door to relieve themselves about a foot away from the door and came right back in. The wet horse blankets hanging about seemed to make the house even colder. It was late afternoon. Just twenty-four hours into this storm and it felt like weeks since I'd been warm, weeks since it all began. I went for water to wash down the sandwich. Nothing from the kitchen faucet. I tried the bathroom with no luck. The pipes weren't frozen; it was almost twenty degrees out.

Who knew that well pumps were electric? I had used up the water in the holding tank and there would be no more. Is this delirium? Would it do any good to panic? Maybe I could melt enough snow. Maybe I could get to the pond with a pick ax and haul from there.

It was starting to get dark, not that I had seen the sun all day. The blizzard howled and roared on without a break in rhythm. There were two spare horse blankets somewhere in the garage and I needed to find them while there was light. I went out the front door to find the garage with the same hand over hand, inching ahead progress. I forced my breath deep and pushed on. Once I made it inside the garage and found the blankets, I considered the shorter walk from here straight to the barn. Close as it was, there was zero visibility. It looked like there might be a drift between the garage and the barn that was higher than my head. Or it was a mirage. I was too frightened to explore. What if I ended up frozen lost, ten feet from the house? How do people survive this in unfamiliar terrain? Hush, that kind of question didn't help.

I dragged the dry blankets back the way I came, then through the house and out the back door to the blown-over path back to the barn. They didn't nicker for me this time. The horses were semi-dry now, and I put the blankets on top of what they already had. Their legs were wet to the bone. Even the stomped-down snow was up to their knees. The snow had filled in almost to the roof, and they had a space not much bigger than two horses to stand in. I couldn't bear looking at them, but Ernest was worse. The snow was deep enough that his chest and belly were submerged, even though he was standing near Spirit. He was wet with every hair slicked down, and shivering so violently that he looked like he was having small convulsions. His eyes were too still. Was he getting hypothermia?

I remembered times at the Leaf River farm when we lost groups of animals to the weather, but I was so little I couldn't remember how they died. It didn't matter right now. Right now this little donkey was looking worse by the minute and the storm showed no hint of letting up. He couldn't stay here and the garage would be impossible to find. I decided to take him to the house, like any donkey in his right mind would leave his herd's barn during a raging blizzard.

Ernest was in no mood to take me at my word. Donkeys always hold to their own opinion above others; we see it as stubborn, they call it smart. His head was low, trying to be invisible to my worry. He knew there was no safer place than next to his big gelding. His breath was ragged; it looked like life or death to me. This storm wore on and he looked a little worse by the minute. Getting him out of the wet was his best chance for survival and we had to go now.

So we started from a place of fundamental disagreement. I dug as much of a path as I could, but the wind had something to say about that. Ernest didn't want his halter on so the nego-tiations began there. The first few steps away from the horses did not go well. I knew better than to pick a big fight and Ernest knew better than to go out of a barn in a storm. Step by step—inch by icy inch. The snowdrifts, when you could see them through the blizzard, were taller than either of us. He stopped each stride and refused to go on. I praised him for each step and asked him to take one more. My words were lost in the wind. He doubted me and I persisted with a controlled, cheerful voice. It was just starting to get dark and the temperature was dropping.

We finally reached the back porch, both of us exhausted, frozen, and in panic denial. The snowdrift by the door had returned. I needed a way to dig the door open and not let Ernest even turn toward the barn. If he got away from me, he might be lost in drifts trying to get back to the horses. Finally I wedged the door as wide as a donkey, but he flatly refused to come in. The porch looked like a small dark hole and the threshold looked scarier to him than the drifts outside. He dug in his heels. I dug in my heels. It wasn't an even match. He weighed 350 pounds and every ounce was leaning back. I did the math—it was a fight I couldn't win.

I got his nose over the threshold and managed to loop the lead rope like a pulley around the doorknob, and then worked my way to his back end without him turning. I put my hips against his rump and pushed. He leaned backward into me with equal pressure. We were united in resistance. I held strong and for more leverage, I put my shoulder to his rump. It got colder by the minute and we each held our ground. I tried to breathe slower and relax my lean without letting up. And he found a way to lean back a bit less, too. I began to rock forward and release. Rock and release. Finally one of his tiny hooves let go of the ground, and he took a tiny half-step forward. Good boy! We rocked on in a bad conga line, getting a bit looser and a bit lighter on our feet, till he crossed the threshold into the porch. Success, but in that split second the sound of his hooves on the wood floor scared both of us. Ernest slipped, lost his balance, and panicked some more. He spun a quick circle to leave, while

I threw my body down to block the door. I had no words, no sounds. Ernest had projectile diarrhea. It happens when he's nervous. Not just a bit, he sprayed watery poop from the dryer to the freezer and across every wall. On the bright side, he'd apparently been drinking plenty and it started to freeze almost immediately, so the odor wasn't bad.

Ernest and I were at eye level now that I was on the ground, so I scratched him a while. His ears were tense and he didn't dare blink. There is just one last doorway and a narrow hall to the laundry room. We could hear the dogs sniffing and whining on the other side of the door. Dogs are natural enemies of donkeys and Ernest liked them best across a fence. I couldn't imagine what else he was hearing and smelling. His eyes were wild but at least the wind wasn't hitting us now. Just a few steps farther; a few more long moments of inching our way and he was in the laundry room. I pulled out the bathroom rug for him to stand on and started to towel him off. His shivering continued for any of a dozen good reasons.

I was so far past exhausted, so weak down to the bone, that it felt like I had reached enlightenment. I floated. I had proved myself more stubborn than a donkey. It was the best I'd felt all day. I tied Ernest to another door knob, and made one more trip to the barn for hay. The path was certainly wider now, in the few places the wind hadn't already blown over.

Ernest reluctantly settled a bit on the bathroom rug as he snacked on hay and I spread more towels on the floor. By the time I fed the dogs and cats, and made another peanut butter sandwich for me, it was almost dark and I could see my breath in the living room. There was still no water. Come morning I'd find a way to melt snow in the powerless, below-freezing world, but for now I had to stop. I found my sleeping bag, rated to minus twenty degrees. Somehow that temperature seemed entirely possible overnight. There was no flashlight but I found a lighter and some candles and put them on the bedside table. Not emergency candles of course, these were scented. Then I zipped deep into the bag, after stuffing three very willing cats inside first. Two more quilts on top, along with Spam and Hero. It was 4:45 in the afternoon of the longest day ever.

When my eyes opened again it was totally dark. I slept hard enough to be disoriented; it was hard to breathe and I felt paralyzed. Then I heard someone was snoring and remembered where I was. The cats and I were sardined together in the mummy bag with the dogs on top. It was toasty warm but also midnight and the horses needed more hay. I layered on my coats and headed out to the barn one more time. The cold was even more cutting with knife-sharp humidity. How was that even possible? Without the yard light, the darkness was absolute; no moon, no stars. No planes, no traffic sounds, only the wind, and now that was quieting to a light, breezy twenty miles per hour. The snow seemed to be blowing up from the ground but it was hard to tell. Spirit and Dodger didn't hear me coming and spooked. They looked embarrassed and miserable. Seeing their wet legs made mine ache in sympathy. There was manure everywhere, very little water left, and the snowdrifts were dense and heavy, and taller than the fence panels on the three open sides. My horses were literally trapped in a snow cave with snowdrifts higher than their heads. I threw too much hay, like that would help. They were stoic; they seemed older and not that enthusiastic about eating. Weather like this stresses their fragile digestive system out of balance. I doled out a light serving of grain, hoping that no one would colic. No vets could find us tonight. I prayed my way back to the house, got back in the sleeping bag, cats on the inside with me, the quilts and dogs piled on top.

My shoulders and my back ached but I didn't let myself think about it. I fought to control my thoughts, so afraid of being swallowed alive by cold fear. If I allowed myself a hint of panic, it might disable me. I was totally overwhelmed, but we all had to push ahead tomorrow. I counted my breaths to steady my mind and slow my heart. I heard Ernest's little hooves in the next room finally come to a rest.

Before the storm I had been reading a book that a friend had given me; a compilation of diaries written by women pioneers on the prairie. These were strong hard-working women whose lives had little comfort and less company. Now I understood the internal emotions of their simple words more profoundly. Their understated style was personal to me; I knew snowbound life-and-death weather. They wrote plain and beautiful descriptions of relentless winter that spread the breadth of the horizon and we were sisters across time.

In one memoir, the writer described the challenges of the cold season bluntly, without emotion or shame. She was alone; her husband had gone to the city to earn a wage while the fields rested over winter. She stayed in their sod house with no windows, present to hold residence on the homestead. If it was found deserted, they would have to homestead again somewhere else. The days passed slowly with no distraction. Eventually the season gave way and she described a man with a wagon who went from homestead to homestead in early spring. He gathered women who had gone cabin-crazy over the winter and took them to the asylum in town. I noticed myself scanning the horizon for that horseman to come from more than a century away. I had previously imagined I wouldn't let him take me, but that was before this storm.

I finally fell into a sleep so deep, so hard, and so thick that my dreams felt like torture. I stumbled and wandered in my sleep, leaning all my weight against the snow. The weight of the covers and my crowded sleeping bag made a cameo appearance. I dreamed I couldn't find the horses. I wandered through several possible outcomes and all of them were bad. When I could not search through snowbanks any more, I found a gap in the dream and pushed into daylight. I woke up hurting and exhausted.

Good news—the sky was clear. The dogs went out the front door just a few feet and relieved themselves and were back in less than a minute. I looked to the east, down the driveway to the road. There were two huge snowdrifts, as deep as my truck was tall, from the ends of my outbuildings on the north side of the farm, all the way to the south fence. With wind that strong, there is no guessing how much snow had actually fallen but it was somewhere between two inches and six feet. The wind-blown drifts intersected my driveway diagonally. In between them was several feet of nearly bare ground. The storm left an extreme all-or-nothing wake of drifts and damage behind. I wouldn't be getting out today.

It was still and silent, nothing was stirring on any of the neighboring properties; no traffic had been down the road. The power was still out. The pasture to the south looked like a barren moon-scape. Any ground cover, grass or weed, had been blown flat. It looked freeze-dried and in some areas almost barren. I hoped to somehow get water for the horses from the pond on the west side, but being lower than the surrounding ground, the entire area was filled with snow with no part of the pond visible. My land was hardly recognizable.

Then I heard a wheezing sound, in and out. It got louder until it erupted. Ernest was trying out an indoor bray. I lost him in my dream but here he was, warm and dry. The laundry room was covered with mud and manure—he had had a little storm of his own there. It was time for breakfast, his eyes were bright, and he was ready to be reunited with the geldings.

Those restless hoof sounds returned. I quickly hooked up a lead rope and we headed out to the back porch. Ernest was anxious but the wind had blown snow to block the door yet again. I had to crack the back door and awkwardly try to shovel it clear from the inside, just enough to get out. I kept a shovel with me now, like some women carry hankies. Behind me was a small donkey who was in a big hurry to get past the dawdling human blocking the door. But Ernest had a certain width about him that would not compromise. It took a few frustrating moments and finally the two of us exploded out the back door.

All we could see of the barn was fence panels coming out of the snowdrifts and an edge of the roof. Ernest wanted to be in front, so I let him break the path. He could see even less of the barn than I could from his height, but he pushed on through snow like a steam engine. A couple of times he got blocked and we traded places so I could shovel, but he pushed ahead of me again at the first chance, rushing to get back to the horses. We circled around and took the human entrance to the barn, pushing along the wall, digging when we needed to. Finally we got to the front of the horse stalls, and the geldings looked okay. Not great, but they were happy to see us. They were in a space that is no bigger than the combined size of their bodies, even more confined than last night.

Where to start digging? It all looked impossible. I took a line near a fence panel, but there was no place to toss the snow away, so I piled it to the side. It was heavy, wet spring snow, so it packed down well. In a little over an hour and a half, I had a path about the width of a horse that was half shoveled and half stomped down. It went steeply up and then sharply down to the paddock of the barn. There were places in the paddock that the wind had blown almost dry and the water tank that still had a few inches of water left.

I tried to encourage the horses out, but after so little warmth or movement, their stiff legs were reluctant. Spirit's eyes looked drawn. They had had a hard night. Dodger was a little more restless in the confinement so I found a halter and lead rope and asked him to follow me. His hooves sank deep on the path and he thrashed a bit. Balance was hard and each step was almost like bucking. He had to rear to lift his front legs clear of the snow but each landing, his hooves slid deep in again. I did my best to get out of his way on the narrow path and he did his best to not land on me as he plowed and hopped his way forward to the sun and open ground on the other side of the drift. I went back for Spirit, knowing that this kind of movement could re-injure his front tendon. He struggled, having much less energy. Slowly, step by step he eventually got clear of the drift. His strides were tentative on the open ground but soon his braced spine relaxed. Each horse dropped and rolled, adjusting their backs on the ground. I felt so much relief watching that I had to lean on a fence to hold myself up. My back was as stiff and stressed as theirs, now that I let myself think about it.

The melting had started. It was spring, after all, and knowing that this wall of snow would be mud soon meant I would be dealing with the aftermath of this storm for quite a while yet. The wind had been a huge dull roar for three days; I'd been braced against the sound of the storm as much as the force of it. And my shoulders eased a bit lower.

Birds were back, just a few. Neighbors began moving around a bit. Best of all, I heard the sounds of a snowplow grunting its way down my little dirt road. I watched it pass, leaving another drift at the end of my driveway. It was so much smaller than the mountainous drifts left by the wind that I didn't mind. It would be a while before I had time to dig the driveway out.

The llamas were next and of course my boots were wet down to my toes, just like my gloves. I was low on replacements so I trudged on ahead to the little barn.

The drift between the horse barn and the little barn was taller with a fine peak on top that slowly tapered as it curved around the shed. The tiny gap that I peered in yesterday had sealed up but I started digging in with the shovel about shoulder high. Would they have oxygen in there? In a few minutes I was near breaking through, when a brown nose poked out from the inside, followed by a couple of curious eyes peering through the gap between the snow and the barn. Sebastian was working on the other side. As soon as there was enough opening to get his shoulder out, he dug his toenails deep and pushed through, followed quickly by the other llamas. The goats climbed immediately to the top of the drift to play King of the Hill. Serious drama is totally lost on goats. A few head butts later the goats scurried along the ridge of the snowdrifts to go visit the horses.

Escape was easy when the fences were buried.

I broke the ice in the llama tank and there was enough water to back up the small amount left in the horse tank. Maybe enough for the day. The power was still out and everything that had gotten wet was staying that way. In the house again, I had a respectable pile of wet socks and gloves. There was no escape from my wet misery. I sat down with some canned peaches and ate them out of the cold can with a cold spoon. My thin veneer of civilization was gone. I spent the rest of the day shoveling paths to the house and around the barn. I got a small start on one of the driveway drifts before my strength gave out. I over-fed the animals and headed for the sleeping bag. The cats were really starting to enjoy this sleeping arrangement. I was almost too tired to sleep after a day of shoveling snow, but I took a cue from the dogs, who snored in a rhythm that rocked my body between them.

Dawn came on my third morning without power. I knew people could survive much worse than this, but I wasn't sure how they did it. I saw a few cars out, and after feeding, I started to dig where the snow-plow had piled my driveway. The snow was frozen hard. As I shoveled, I devised a route to zig-zag between some of the drifts and over others, hoping the open ground between the diagonal drifts of snow would power me over the deeper, but barely shoveled-out drifts. I might be able to 4-wheel it around other drifts by going through the pasture, and if I could clear the nasty part at the end of the driveway, it could work. After a couple more hours of shoveling I was ready to give it a try. I started the truck to let it warm up and cranked up the heat. It was sheer luxury. Why hadn't I thought of this sooner? Then I wove my truck between drifts and fish-tailed over top of others. Once I got toward the end of the drive, I gunned the truck's big American engine and hit the partly dug-out track hard. No luck. I backed up farther and this time, incorporated a last minute spin of the steering wheel. If I didn't make it, I would wipe out the gate, the fence, and some part of my truck's front end but it would be worth it. I revved up like a dragster and dropped it into gear. The truck spun, skidded, bumped and eventually flung itself out onto the icy-slick road.

I tried to ignore that nasty burning smell coming from the engine while I drove the short three miles into populated civilization. The air cleared by the time I got to the central intersection and the bank sign displayed the time. They had power here. I drove past the feed store to the Carhartt Cafe. That wasn't the real name; I gave it the nickname because there was a dress code there. I saw a couple of cars and slid into the parking lot.

Places like this always have a community table with a few ranchers or farmers drinking coffee. It's timeless. My father took me along when I was a kid and ordered me the unique delicacy of buttered toast. They used sliced bread.

On this day, I scurried past the men with my eyes on the floor and took a booth. As I started to peel off layers, the waitress came to my table with a menu and the coffee pot. I could smell its heat and my arm caught in the sleeve of my coat. Then she said those impossibly sweet and magical words, "Coffee, Honey?" I pushed my cup toward her, and before I could say please, the tears started. Not just sniffles, it was my trademark loud barking snot-filled sobs. Like other times in my life, I was strong as I need to be, right up until someone said something nice. I tolerate pain so much easier than kindness.

The waitress put her hand on my heaving shoulder as she poured my coffee and asked, "Did you have a hard time getting out?"

The men at the other table stared at their cups, embarrassed by my outburst. I had some quaint idea of how I looked to them but absolutely no way to control it. I ordered breakfast in the middle of the afternoon, "Eggs, hash browns, two orders of bacon. Everything very hot, please." She refilled my coffee twice before my plate came. I tipped her twice the bill when I left. Caffeine, bacon and an angel-waitress made me whole. The power was back on when I got home.

A Member of the Wedding

When Sebastian was five years old, he was asked to participate in a wedding. The bride had known him for a while and he was especially fond of her. She had deep auburn hair and golden skin. He was always drawn to warm complexions—she was his type.

Seb was the llama who was famous for "kissing" at the National Western Stock Show when he was young. I had taken a couple of llamas to show and his reputation seemed to spread magically by word of mouth. All day long people showed up at his stall and asked, "Is this the kissing llama?" By mid-afternoon, I wasn't flattered anymore. I was tired, but Sebastian was not. I stopped going into the pen and instead, I sent strangers in alone.

"Yes, go on in. Keep your hands at your side," I said. Unfailingly, he stopped eating and raised his ears, as if this unique person was the most interesting and beautiful person in the world. He leaned close to smell their breath and then wiggled his nose with a soft mumble. The visitors were spellbound, each one thinking they were special. He took his job as good will ambassador seriously.

So, when he was asked to be ring bearer for this wedding, I agreed and didn't think much about it. I knew he would love it. Of course I made him a matching cummerbund. I think that's the approved wedding apparel for llamas. The wedding was a couple of hours away in the Colorado Mountains. I splurged and rented a van so we didn't have to take the truck and trailer.

Besides, we didn't need much room. We packed our good clothes, a few dogs, and snacks for all of us. Sebastian stepped right in and found a good place to cush in back, and we were off. Sebastian was always up for a trip. He didn't mind separating from the herd and was endlessly curious and very polite.

The remote mountain resort where the wedding was being held was at the end of a winding road through a pine forest. The parking area had more trees than cars and just beyond was a gracious log and stone lodge with an inviting front porch that ran the length of the building. The wedding party stayed in log cabins that were sprinkled through the trees and a white tent was ready for the reception. What I particularly loved about the place was the outdoor spot where the actual ceremony would take place. There were rows of would-be pews; logs split in half as benches with an aisle down the center. In front there was a huge, rustic log archway that had the abstract shape of a church. It framed a huge meadow that tapered in the distance in between two snow-capped mountains. A dozen horses grazed in tall grass and wildflowers. The breeze ambled through stands of Aspen trees. Hundreds of acres felt intimate and sacred. It was meant to reflect a church without walls.

When I was still living at home, I made the decision to leave the Catholic faith. It took courage. It was a spiritual life-or-death decision, with the threat of eternal damnation hanging in the air. It seemed to my teen-aged mind that the priests were more interested in being intolerant and judgmental than loving and caring about people. Instead, on Sunday mornings I walked in the woods, singing or giving myself a sermon about living a good life. I found God outside and animals were an intrinsic part of that. It was both simple and profound, it was my safe haven. When I saw this church with no walls, and the arch framing a view of nature, I knew it was created by someone like me. Someone who perhaps saw God reflected in the natural world more than the human world.

As the ceremony time drew near, I met the minister and

found out more wedding details. The couple didn't have friends standing up with them, so the only other participant in the ceremony was Sebastian. (And me.) We got the rings and stood to the side, next to a colorful, old-fashioned sort of floral arrangement that Sebastian watched with hungry eyes. The pews filled with family and friends. The bride arrived in a traditional white dress that somehow looked magical in the forest. When it was time, we both walked over to join the couple.

As the first ring was given with a heartfelt vow, it was touching and emotional. When the bride turned to get the second ring, there was a tear in the corner of her eye. Sebastian saw it and very gently leaned forward and put his lips to her brow. It was a sweet, affectionate sort of movement, the bride softly laughed with a tilt to her head. The groom had a giant smile and everyone sighed or laughed or clapped. In the love of the moment, Sebastian had done what everyone watching hoped they would do in his place. The second ring was given with its vow and more happy tears. We stepped back to the side and by the end of the ceremony we all felt beautifully married.

I took Sebastian back to the van and gave him some hay, and went to the reception. No one was happy to see me without my date and the bride asked me to go get him. There was food and dancing, tables to sit at. It was kind of crowded and people can be unpredictable, but I went out and got him. Everyone greeted Seb like an old friend and I sipped wine with a llama on my arm. He was the most polite of company, and all the women loved him. There was that one incident when Seb nibbled the Mother-of-the-Groom's corsage, which he mistook for an hors d'oeuvres. It was an easy mistake to make and no one panicked.

Sebastian's eyes followed a beautiful blond woman. She had an accent from Texas, her hair was *yella*, and she wore a matching low-cut *yella* sun dress that might have been a size too small. Or maybe she was just larger than life. She had honey-tanned skin, moist and rich with freckles that looked like an old photo in Kodacolor. I notice all these intimate details because I know my llama. The Texas woman was perfect, his dream girl, and he would eventually need some of her breath.

Sebastian was not the only one to notice the woman; she had the eye of several older men there as well. They looked at her with raised eyebrows, they smiled when she laughed, and their body language was deferential. She was the sort of woman who held a llama's eye and made old men wish they were young again.

I did not seek her out; it was inevitable that the mingling would bring us together. She was bubbly and bright, and her musical laugh hung in the air. Finally it happened. We were standing behind her and she turned right into us. Sebastian's eyes widened. He was mesmerized. She said a few words that he didn't hear, as he slowly leaned forward and gently inserted his face between her ear and her hair and didn't move. She held her breath, silent and looking at me for a sign. Every man watching held his breath with her. Sebastian let out a sigh. At that moment, all the men liked Sebastian, too.

"He likes you." I said, speaking for everyone who admired that particular shade of *yella.*

Why I Like Ducks

There was a hen-house at the farm on Leaf River. It was a small shed with laying boxes along one wall and chicken ladders for roosting. Yellow straw bedding padded the boxes to protect eggs and was flung on the ground to catch droppings. On the opposite wall, there was a chicken-sized door that opened onto the scratch yard. I was five years old and the chickens were mainly my responsibility.

In the morning my first job was to feed the chickens out in their scratch pen. When they saw me they came running, all clucked-up loud and flapping their wings. Potato peels, other left-over vegetables, bread scraps, and a coffee can of grain were all tossed together on the ground for the hens to search and nibble. Potato peels were their favorite and since we ate potatoes every day, the chickens were never disappointed. Most of the hens left their eggs to meet me outside for breakfast, so it was an easier time to gather eggs. I collected one or two eggs from each box. If the egg was still warm, I held it to my cheek for a moment. Eggs are such wondrous objects. Some of the hens were broody; they had an enlarged commitment to procreation and fiercely protected their eggs, as scary as a pit bull with a wing span. I was probably more afraid of those broody hens than any of the big animals on the farm. They tilted their heads glaring at me with pointy beaks and beady eyes, and I had to go eyeball to eyeball with them to snake my hand under their bottoms and take their warm eggs away. Hysterical clucking, flapping, and pecking were all part of the daily life-and-death struggle to bring in the eggs.

There was constant adjustment to the flock. Some hens got pecked to death and others found a way to escape and got eaten by predators. Chickens don't lay forever and once they're old, they aren't so good for eating, so their life span was "managed." Some new birds came home from the feed store each spring. Each fall our freezer was stuffed with Sunday dinners stored ahead.

The freezer didn't fill magically. It was usually considered women's work to butcher chickens. My sister and I caught the chickens and held them upside down by their feet while my mother swung the heavy iron cleaver high and hacked heads off on the block. She tossed the chickens off to the side before grabbing another from our hands. The headless chicken bodies ran and flapped for a brief moment and once they stopped I rounded them all up. Then my mother dipped them in a giant kettle of boiling water to scald them so they were easier to pluck. There were feathers everywhere, but plucking wasn't my job. I had the smallest hand so gutting was my job. Chickens fueled my nightmares back then; if it wasn't getting my eyes pecked out, it was my mother with the cleaver.

I hadn't had a chicken dream in decades; fresh eggs sounded great and I didn't own a cleaver. I was past all that. Then one day at the feed store I heard tiny peeps. I did some quick math and when all was said and done, I figured with feed, and not butchering, the eggs would cost five or six times the cost of organic eggs at the grocery. That worked for me, but broody chickens can make you feel like you're fighting a daily war of survival, stealing their unborn children. I looked at the ducklings. They quacked a nicer tune. Ducks needed a pool and that meant mud and flies and all, but still, no pointy beaks.

It was a small start, four tiny ducklings under a light in a cardboard box. The next problem was where they would live when they moved outside. The farm was surrounded by predators, not to mention neighbor dogs. Ducks would need protecting so I built a duck pen inside of the llama pen. There was a small entry so ducks could waddle inside but the goats couldn't get in and steal the duck chow. That task took months of re-working because the goats were very persistent. But the llamas kept predators away and when the ducks weren't using the pool, the llamas could cool their toes. It was a complete little eco-system of a sort.

It would be hard to find a less serious species than ducks. They quack to high heaven day or night, flap ferociously in group hysteria if frightened or happy or they want fresh water in the pool. They mated all the time. Including during ground blizzards. Sure enough, each of the ducks had a definite personality. One female was much smarter than the rest, a genius by duck standards. She always found the food first and knew where water was. She would have been a great leader if the boys weren't so puffed up about themselves. Instead, she got beat up a lot and I had to get good at duck first aid.

There was no egg drama at all. They left them for me out in the middle of the pen like stray rocks. Sometimes I saw a female plop out the most beautiful blue-green egg without breaking stride or looking back. They must have hatched eggs at some point, but these girls were no more interested in motherhood than I was. Delicious guilt-free eggs, if you got them before the llamas walked on them or the dogs ate them.

I didn't take the ducks very seriously at first but they became part of our herd. I chatted with them, thanked them for the eggs and tried to cajole them inside their house during storms. They were wild for frozen peas.

Eventually only two ducks were left. Fred and Ethel had lived so long that there were no more eggs to gather, no more orgies in the middle of the night. Still, they remained devoted to each other. Ethel was small and brown and Fred loudly defended and protected her. They were never apart. If Fred got too far ahead, he would march in place until Ethel caught up with him, both of them quacking with relief that they were together again.

One day there was a break-out. Fred and Ethel escaped the

safety of the llama pen and found the pond. Oh, joy! It was an ocean to them. Coyotes drop by the pond regularly for duck snacks and Fred and Ethel were elderly, so I herded them back to the barn. It ends up that you can get attached to these silly birds.

But bright and early the next day, Fred and Ethel escaped again. They waddled as fast as they could toward the pond, quacking hysterically at their cleverness. I think Ethel was limping a bit, but it's hard to tell with ducks. They launched onto the pond and immediately looked like decoys. They were larger and they swam too low in the water; they couldn't hoist their bottoms up like the wild ducks. So they kept apart, happy with each other and a few pond bugs. If the wild ducks came too close, Fred would flap and quack and move them back. He was chivalrous that way and Ethel gave a deep low quack to thank him.

Around evening feeding time, Fred and Ethel would come back to the barn and share supper with Spirit. He tossed a bit of his grain down to them. I tried to duck-proof the pen, but every day they found a way out, sometimes heading out the front driveway to double back in a long arc through the pasture and finally the pond. That's a big plan for a duck. I gave up containing them, in favor of a quicker return if they got chased. For the next year domestic duck life on the pond was very good and Fred and Ethel had the best of both worlds.

But one day Fred was frantically scurrying from pen to pond and back again, muttering in a lost, worried way. It was unimaginable that Ethel was gone. I looked for her with him but there was no sign. I felt sure that Half-Tail had gotten her. Fred mourned long and deep. He went to the pond but marched right back. He couldn't seem to settle.

But Fred survived his mourning period. He still went to the pond with dedicated stride and I worried until he came back for supper. We all watched out for him, even the goats seemed to keep an eye on him. He commandeered a stall in the barn for the winter and we were glad for his comfort.

That next spring when the pond thawed, something caught my eye. Instead of the usual cliques on the pond, Fred's distinctive, low outline was in the middle of a flotilla of wild ducks. It wasn't perfect—he still couldn't lift his backside in the air. But he'd made friends with the wild ducks and they seem to like him, too. He eventually went back to his old bossy self around the barn, lovable as ever.

Seeing Fred find his place on the pond made me so grateful for second chances. Lots of us have to start our lives over when we don't expect it—dogs, horses, and people too. It takes courage to launch again and a cheer from friends on the shore can make all the difference.

Before moving to the farm, my midlife crisis had a grisly feel of a summer blockbuster movie with big screen special effects: Car chases. Explosions. Death. Cleavers. Everything was over the top.

Life on the farm became more like an independent film: Slow. Heartfelt. Small. Why would anyone care about the insignificant lives of two old ducks? Is the quality of a life judged by the ones not living it? Is an emotion limited by who feels it? In the course of the world, my life isn't any bigger than an old duck's. He was as good a teacher as any. I had to stoop over to listen, but he let me know that humanity wasn't relegated strictly to humans.

The Wild Texas Wind

Naturally my herd of horses grew. How could it not? Dodger was going strong, but Spirit was starting to show his age at seventeen. He'd had arthritis for a few years and recently he'd injured his tendon again. It meant months on stall rest and in the time it took the tendon to heal, Spirit's arthritis had run wild. His back was swayed and he looked elderly. It was a forced retirement. Spirit became my Grandfather Horse, not what either of us wanted.

My fiftieth birthday was on the horizon and I began looking for my next dressage horse. That was the first time I met Windy. The Wild Texas Wind was her name and she was in the background, the dam of a weanling I looked at. She seemed to share my wonder at her colt as he glided a trot with his hooves barely touching the ground. Windy was a chestnut mare of an average height and an average conformation. She was quiet, she didn't stand out. When her colt, Nubè, came to my barn a few months later, I heard she was sold off to a breeder in the northern part of Colorado.

I didn't think about her again until a couple of years later. I heard the owners of the breeding farm had run into health problems and their herd had to be sold off quickly. I knew there wasn't much of a market for an older broodmare who wasn't ride-able. That probably meant she would go to an auction, followed by a terrifying ride on a crowed transport to slaughter in Mexico. Maybe I hoped that someone would return the favor for me one day if I was in need. Whatever, Windy was family.

I bought her for a killer's price and hauled her home. She was understated in her reactions, too. She seemed to almost recognize my barn, more so than her grown colt. She was nervous but trying not to make a fuss about it.

In the next few weeks, we got acquainted with each other. Windy was distrusting and hard to catch. She carried some level of anxiety almost all the time. I didn't blame her for not making a great first impression; she had been passed around. Most likely only caught for vet work and nothing else—not the best interaction with humans. Windy was past her prime and she didn't ask for much. I told her she was really home this time.

The next year I decided to breed her to the stallion that sired Nubè, my young gelding. No, the world did not need any more horses. I knew there were more than a few going to slaughter already. I never wanted children, and all my dogs and cats were spayed or neutered. I had no plans to get fabulously rich breeding horses. I knew a foal would only cost me money. It was an informed family-planning decision that I didn't take lightly. No one got accidentally pregnant on my watch. And I was selfish. I wanted a foal born on my farm and Windy got the work she loved best; being a stay-at-home mom.

In the breeding world, they are prone to talk about the sires more than the mares. My sire of choice was a tall, lanky Andalusian stallion. He was all heart and try, a Grand Prix Dressage horse who was a sheer joy to ride, even in retirement. It would be easy to miss this quiet mare in the background, but the more I got to know Windy through the pregnancy, the more I could see what she contributed to my gelding, Nubè. She was almost serene, so smart, and had such lovely kind eyes. Mare eyes, we call them; soft and deep as her heart.

Windy put a rosy glow on most days during her pregnancy. On long Indian Summer afternoons, we grazed and curried and watched her belly grow. Winter passed and she and I became fast friends. She was shy but not frightened anymore. She and Spirit had become inseparable.

Then a month before Windy was due to deliver, she began to colic. It was the result of a vet giving a shot that I had declined. *Declined means no!* The vet shrugged when I confronted her. "It happens," she said.

I watched in disbelief as my mare flinched in pain and fear. The unborn foal kicked and fought inside. Colic is the number one killer of horses, and I take it very seriously.

The vet gave Windy some pain meds in the hope they would relax her enough to ease the colic but with no success. I wanted to strangle the vet when she told me to haul her to the clinic in Denver for surgery. I took a deep breath and told the truth. "Windy is not a surgery candidate," I choked. I had to choose the possible death sentence. If Windy survived the two-hour trip and then the challenging surgery, the foal would make it all so much more complicated, if it survived at all. Beyond that, I would still have to find a way to pay. I simply did not have the money.

The vet told me that the foal was too premature to deliver. Like I didn't know that. Like she hadn't caused this incident with her unwanted vaccination.

As her truck pulled out, I didn't waste more energy on the vet. I walked Windy to keep her on her feet, one hand on her neck and counting my inhales to keep my breath slow. I was terrified of losing her and her foal.

As the hours passed, we came to know each other's mettle and courage. The pain never lessened but we took turns being strong. It was heartbreaking to see her look around to her flank. Little hooves kicked visibly and Windy had to be tired. I loved this mare, but seeing her strength now made my heart explode with respect and awe. We fought on for the foal. I worked pressure points that I knew, massaging her belly and hind until the pain inside was too much for Windy to stand still. Then we walked a circle or two and tried to rest again.

Hours passed and finally I just couldn't keep her on her feet any longer. She wanted to lie down. If she thrashed, she might twist her intestines and that would be the end. I would lose them both, but I decided to trust her. There was no other choice. On the ground her huge belly looked even more painful. The foal was still kicking inside of her and she felt no relief. I forced my breath slower and more deliberate for her baby. It was all I could do.

Windy struggled to her feet again, unbalanced by her huge belly. We walked a couple of minutes and she went down again with a thud. She got up and down a couple more times. She didn't thrash but it didn't help either. Then in an instant, her eyes changed. It was just that quick. She must have managed to release what was binding her and the baby up inside. She blew hard through her nostrils. That's horse for *I feel relaxed*. Her flanks went soft as the baby relaxed inside. She started looking for some hay and I sat down hard.

My other horse partnerships had always been under saddle. Windy and I had no weekend horse shows, no winning rides. This mare took me somewhere just as deep—a trial by fire. It made the salon-boy geldings look like wimps. Caring for Windy the last month of her pregnancy was a time of sharing something that was so blood-red female, so filled with sacred magic, that I was totally disarmed by it.

The spring weather was unseasonably warm. Each day Windy got rounder and bigger and each day my heart swelled a bit more. I let her waddle around on the lawn, I gave her special snacks. She returned each kindness with such sweet nuzzles. I made her a private area in the pen with soft bedding. I put plywood up along the stall so the foal wouldn't get hung up in the fence panel bars. The run was in full view from the window in the guest bedroom so I slept there at night. She wandered to the corner of the pen and watched me and if I raised my hand in acknowledgment, she nickered back.

The afternoon came when Windy told me tonight would be the time. She didn't hide; she leaned close and I could see the baby restless to be born. All the physical signs confirmed it. She was so soft, so beautiful, not at all the defensive frightened mare who first came. I put extra shavings in her stall and wrapped her tail and followed that with a soft massage. She was in labor when I finally went into the house. The contractions were easy to see. I lay on the guest bed and looked out the window, she looked back.

Around midnight she began pacing and I knew the time was close. She lay down. She got up. Finally she stayed down and soon I saw some little feet, and then some wet ears. I waited until the baby was on the ground; she knew what she was doing and I gave her that respect. Then I pulled on my coat and went out.

It was a full moon on the prairie, as light as day. My other horses were all straining over the fence to see the baby, all anxious to say hello. Windy nickered me in to meet this baby. It was a little filly, shy but very strong. The filly was cautious so I gave her some space. We would have years to get to know each other. I scratched Windy and together we admired the first and only baby born on my farm, by the light of the moon, a miracle. We named her Claro d' Luna—Moonlight.

Time for imprinting the filly, nicknamed Clara. Horses have strong memory and the first 24 hours are a time to introduce the youngster to her future life. Once she had nursed and was dry, I was ready with halter, clippers, and brushes but Windy beat me to it. She started moving the filly and I watched. Windy gave the master class in imprinting. She taught so much with such precision, that I just stood back and learned. Windy taught Clara the important skills: To be brave and polite. I just haltered her and picked up feet. I was grateful to be there. Watching this miracle unfold from the beginning had been beautiful, but she included me in the process. I felt like her family, her support. And now, as we watched the filly frolic, we stood with our shoulders touching, just so very proud.

Some animal people refer to themselves as a dog mom or a horse mom. I didn't do it then and would never do that when

Clara was older. I knew her mother and I was no-where near that good.

Windy never asked for special treatment. She was the last to eat, she stood back and waited her turn. Each tiny acknowledgment from me meant so much, she seemed almost too grateful for any crumb of attention. Never the trouble maker, she was the Mom. She took care of others first. She could always be found with her muzzle at Spirit's hip every day, literally in his shadow, the very best of friends. And the Grandfather Horse was mesmerized by the filly. Our herd thrived.

As the full-moon filly, Clara, grew up and years passed, Windy's health started to change. Her estrous cycles had always been troublesome but now they tormented her. In the last few months she had grown a bit distant. She was uncomfortable most of the time and I knew she had some health issues common for mares her age; that life was beginning to catch up with her. She held a good weight but she colicked in October. I gave her and the Grandfather Horse a full month of sand purge. Old horses are more prone to have sand in their colon and the drought that year had put us in a dust bowl reality. But I wasn't certain that was the whole story.

Another colic six weeks later, but smaller, the vet said. I never think colic is small or easy. They are all painful for the horse. Some do resolve by themselves but it can all turn bad in a moment. Small colic is only an opinion available in hindsight. Sand was the culprit again. How did she ingest so much in such a short time? Windy was on the ground and still. Clearly in pain, but no thrashing. She was flat down with her eyes closed and her breathing was a bit tense. Everyone else was eating except her. I called the vet out quickly and he gave the usual meds. Only slightly dehydrated, Windy got through it, but I kept thinking about her symptoms. I've seen lots of colic. Sadly I'm good at reading pain in these silent creatures. I read her face, but her response this time was to lie down and surrender.

Windy was sick again in three weeks. There was a big shift in weather, a storm front with big wind and temperature swings. It was colic weather, but no one said it out loud. Windy was slightly off. She would eat a bite and lie down. No thrashing or drama, just down at unusual times of the day and not quite right. Each horse had a way of being that became second nature to me; it was always easy to tell when someone was a not well. Two days passed and she wasn't better or worse.

By midday the third day, Windy went downhill fast. I couldn't get her on her feet. Again, I didn't see the overt pain, the thrashing that was expected, but her eyes were tense. I could tell she hadn't eaten all morning. She wasn't well and she wasn't fighting it. The vet arrived and did his check-up. Windy was very dehydrated and there were no gut sounds, but he could hear sand. All bad signs. How could she be full of sand again? He told me that if she survived this colic, she would need to wear a muzzle and live on stall mats. Off the dirt. I knew that wouldn't be an easy life for any horse, confined and alone, but extra hard on an arthritic old mare who loved her arthritic old gelding friend. Horses never do anything by accident. In the wild, horses wander to find the nutrients they crave like salt and minerals. I had to think she was self-medicating another ailment by eating all this dirt.

The vet began the conversation about euthanizing her. This colic pattern was repetitive and it wasn't the first time I thought of the possibility. Surgery was perhaps possible but risky and the outcome not guaranteed. Her age and condition didn't make her a good candidate.

My sweet mare would have gone to the killers in the beginning if I hadn't brought her home. She always asked for so little for herself—she waited her turn forever and unfailingly said thank you. Windy was just good, so much better than me. I wanted to go back to the night Clara was born, to the birth side of this circle of life. But she wasn't thinking about the past; not thinking of babies or stallions or even me. She was in the moment, inside of herself, and she was serene. Her breath was short, her heart rate was up, but she was peaceful. How much did she want to fight? Temperatures were dropping fast; I had to choose.

I had known so many people who turn older animals into science projects trying to save them from old age. Was there a contest about who could make an animal live twice its lifespan? It isn't a crime to live a long life, get old, and die. My head spun back and forth.

I thought of my father, a hard man who killed animals as a matter of course. He died slowly from cancer. At one point he told me he was thinking of killing himself. I guess I understood that choice, since his best days weren't ahead of him. I told him he would not get judgment from me on that. A month later he was too sick to arrange it, and he asked me to help. I told him that I couldn't, and for once he didn't fight my opinion. In a moment of rare understanding and respect between us, he said, "If I was a dog, you could put me down."

Do we put loved ones, human or animals, through painful or un-natural medical procedures until they all fail just because we can't let them go? Do we make them feel like a failure in the process? Big questions in the human world, but having the choice for our animals doesn't make it much easier. When we separate them from the natural circle of life to an extreme, are we somehow disrupting their fate or trying to fool Mother Nature? Why are we reluctant to set them free? My biggest question in this pile of questions, the one I think matters the most: What do *they* want? What did Windy want?

I made two lists in my mind. One list had all of Windy's good deeds and my love for her, the many hearts who loved her, my gratitude for her friendship and the intense female intimacy we had shared. She was the heart of our family. There was love, but even more than that was respect. This mare's life mattered.

The second list had all of her physical conditions and chronic health issues. She was an old mare. Her best days weren't ahead of her either. How many of these colic episodes could we save her from? Why did they recur so often? I pictured her future quality of life in a muzzle on stall mats. The less she moved the worse the pain of her arthritis, all the while seeing her herd out grazing. How punishing was that? Then I asked myself if this condition, or this decision, would be any different if I had all the money in the world.

My mind spun frantically. The vet was patient, but I knew Windy was hurting. I checked my mental lists again. And then I shut up the chatter in my head and looked deep into her sweet eyes. My throat closed like a fist. She was the quiet one who spoke volumes. I inhaled and listened hard. My gut tightened and I pushed the inhale even deeper. I forced myself calm and listened deeper. I didn't want her to give up. And I didn't want to give her up.

I looked in her eye. *It's okay.* It felt like good-bye and I didn't trust it. Another breath, my pleading eye to her peaceful eye. *It's all okay.* And somehow I knew beyond a doubt she was ready. This time I did trust it and a flood of love followed. Emergencies bring clarity sometimes. It's an impossibly heartbreaking moment when life twists itself around far enough that death looks like a blessing.

"I want to let her go."

I looked at her when I said it. She was standing close and sweet. I had a loose lead rope over my shoulder, one of my hands on her forehead and other on her shoulder. She was serene.

My vet asked me where we should go. We would want her in an area that a truck could come to remove her body easily, with gate access. Yes, we were talking logistics at a time like this. Would separating her from the horses be hard on her? Hard on them? I took a guess. By the tree in the south pasture—she loved it there. The vet told us to start the walk and he would get the drugs from the truck and meet us there. Windy and I turned toward the pasture moving slowly and I could hear the other horses get restless. Was Windy going to turnout in the pasture? Would they go, too?

Lately, she walked slowly on a good day, but today we took very small steps. If Windy heard the other horses, she didn't mind. Was she partway gone already? I breathed a long slow inhale and exhaled through my mouth. It was horses who taught me that breath was connection. Windy's breath was shallow, so I expanded it with mine. "Good girl, good mom." She was our matriarch. She was mine. We walked through the gate to the pasture, and the wind picked up. The second half of this storm front was here and the sun was cooling down fast.

My young vet was respectful. He said we could take the time we needed. She was wearing her winter blanket, and he asked if I wanted to take it off. "No, let's leave it on."

The vet explained the process, but I knew it by heart, remembering dogs and cats and other horses who I shared this moment with. "Euthanizing is not always predictable." I'd been here enough that I knew more than I wanted to. "Horses are large and you can't predict how they will fall." And they fall hard, it's a memorable sound. I'd hold her head for him during the injection and if she fell, I'd be ready to step back. Sometimes it's hard to get both syringes in, but that was necessary. If she fell to the ground, I would have to hold her head high enough for him to finish. I'd had that unforgettable experience, too, I understood.

The syringes were ready. The needle is very large and the liquid is hot pink, not a color you would mistake for another drug, not a color that you forget.

Windy was serene. She was fine. So I took my cue from her. I found a calmness in her that I could share. This is how it is with horses, some days they carry you and some days you carry them. I knew we were partners, that she trusted me. In this precious moment there was a gift I could give her: I could give her freedom. I said we were ready.

He moved to the big vein in her neck and inserted the needle and tested. A bit of blood should draw back in the top of the syringe when the needle found the vein. Windy was calm, we were sharing breath. I said it then, like I said it every day, "Good girl, nothing but good." He repositioned the needle again and again. He thought it was going right through her vein, that the vein was flat. Her big sweet heart is not so strong right now. "So good, so very good," I wanted those words in her ear. He apologized and went to the other side to try that vein. Somehow as the wind blew around us peacefully, we were all right.

He tried the needle again and after a couple of tries, found the vein. The first syringe was injected, he held the needle in the vein, tossed that first empty syringe to the ground as I handed him the second. The hand-off was smooth and she slumped to the ground as he finished. He warned me again that she might gasp or kick. But I could see her eye and there was peace. I smoothed her face, as calm now as it was a moment ago. "My sweet girl, so good." I knew she was gone, with her consent and our help.

We waited with her body, listening for a moment with his stethoscope. The vet and I were both relieved that the process had been smooth. It was then that I heard Clara scream. She screamed hot and hard and she didn't stop. She was throwing a raging fit of bucking and kicking, in utter panic. Would she break down the fence? Would she hurt herself? Her brother in the next pen caught her fear and ran and bucked with her. Everyone was wide-eyed except Spirit. The Grandfather Horse knew.

The vet and I walked back to the barn. While he went to stow his gear in the truck, I took a tarp over to cover Windy's body. I tucked it under her head and around her hooves, as respectfully as I could manage. She was lovely even now, so fearless.

Back at the barn, Clara was over-stressed and over-heated. The storm was visible as it came up the valley. I moved Spirit into Clara's pen. It was much too big with Windy gone. Everyone there, down to the last goat, watched me. I threw both hay and alfalfa and told all of them they were good one more time.

At the truck, my vet said they would send the bill and I

signed papers. This young vet was relatively new to the practice. We took stock of each other that day and it was good. He was touched by Windy, though I can't imagine this part of his job ever gets easier. I love a vet who lets his heart show. He pulled down the driveway and I looked at the tarp again. It was holding in the wind. Some folks bury their horses on their farms but I'm pragmatic; it's a small farm. I knew the best part of my red mare was gone and there was ground water to think about. I called the number my vet left and said that I needed Windy to be picked up. "I'm sorry for your loss, ma'am." Ache, it just ached, this love so beautiful and ugly. My eyes returned to the tarp.

The man with the big truck arrived within the hour, parked out on the road and walked up to the house. He saw the tarp. Again, with his hat in his hand, "So sorry for your loss." He looked like Santa Claus in Carhartts, I wanted to hug him. Instead, I showed the good sense of going into my house. I've stood guard over bodies being loaded; they use a winch and drag the body onto the trailer. My eyes had seen enough today. He returned in a few moments. She was loaded and I had the check ready. He handed me Windy's winter blanket neatly folded. "Thank you, ma'am." His kindness gripped my heart.

In the barn Clara was exhausted and the pens were finally quiet. I mucked to settle my mind. Mucking is the miracle cure for most kinds of distress but this time it didn't work. We all looked for Windy. It was easy to identify her manure piles. She had chronic diarrhea for the last two years but I wasn't ready to pick those up yet. In the weeks that followed, the whole herd came apart. The Grandfather Horse got depressed and didn't eat well. Clara seemed to go through all the stages of grief; she was angry and sullen—impatient with all of us. The other horses kind of wandered and didn't know where to be. She was our Boss Mare but she was so quiet about it that we didn't know how much we all depended on her until she was gone.

In Cars with Drunks

I'm sure Windy would want to be remembered with a baby at her side. They were precious to her in a way that I had never felt. I'm not sure my mother ever felt it either. My mother lived with such anxiety, always arranging her resources to their best advantage, always trying to survive. I think that's how it became a habit to send me off in cars with drunks.

My mother had a brother who visited us. My uncle was a small, balding man with a gnarly look and a huge horse-shoe-shaped scar on his forehead. Even when I was young I thought it was probably from a drunken fall. He'd lost his family and several jobs to alcoholism. He'd lost everything except the ability to manipulate my mother. They talked in secret voices in the kitchen when my father was at work. My mother nervously defended him at every opportunity.

Our family didn't keep liquor in the house so when that uncle came to visit he always said he had an errand to run and borrowed our car. Mom knew where he was going, which is why she sent me along with him. It was always the same; my uncle talked big about buying presents for his estranged daughters, but instead he drove straight to a bar. I was in grade school and felt awkward all the time anyway, but still, this was different. Every time he borrowed the car, I fought going along.

"Please, don't make me," I said. My mother had to pull me by my wrist out to the car.

"You're being silly, you don't want to make him feel bad, do you?" It felt so creepy to me. Creepy was the only word I had for it.

Bars were always dark in the middle of the day. My uncle bought me a Coke while he drank beer with whiskey chasers. We sat at the bar so he'd have someone to talk to. He chain smoked and told dirty jokes to the bartender. After each punchline he snorted phlegm to the back of his throat and laughed harder than anyone listening. Sometimes he looked at me perched on the stool next to him but I perpetually pretended to be looking at something in the distance.

Did he think I didn't understand dirty jokes? Drunks always think kids have no awareness and sometimes it was smart to go along. I watched this adult world; others looking at him but never at me. Was I invisible? And my child's mind always asked the same question: Was this normal? Everyone—my mother, the bartender, the other patrons—acted like it was the most ordinary outing. But there were no other kids there. It felt funny inside; I didn't trust them.

Two or three hours later, he was drunk enough that the good ol' boy veneer began to fray. My uncle's voice got louder and more animated until he'd slam his fist down and swear, "God damn, son-of-a-bitch!" at another drunk loud enough to get asked to leave. Other times he broke glasses or just ran out of money.

"Come on, George," he said. Why did he call me a boy's name? Then he'd push up to his feet, snorting and unsteady, and pull me close and lean on my shoulder, mumbling his way back to the car. I dreaded this part. I tried to make eye contact with as many people as I could. *Look at this! Is this normal? Can you see me?* No one met my pleading eyes, no one stopped us. People carefully looked away.

The bar seemed to get quiet as we left but maybe it was just that my uncle was done talking loud. He got behind the wheel and started the car. I told him how to get out of the parking lot. I think this was why mom wanted me there, so he could find his way back.

At some point on the way home he always swerved to a stop

and his skin got blood red as his eyebrows squeezed together and the tears started. He looked like his head would pop. My uncle told me for the hundredth time that he missed his wife and children.

"I'm sorry, George. You're just a kid," he'd apologize, as his head fell to my shoulder. More gasps and sobs came as he told me again how much he missed his family. As he sobbed, his head fell into my lap, heavy and wet. I had no idea what to do, so I sat as still as I could and tried to hold my breath. All the adults acted like this was normal enough; I was the only one who got creeped out. He smelled like rubbing alcohol.

Now I am older than my mother was then. I still don't understand. I wouldn't let my dog into a drunk's car. Every year before Mother's Day the airwaves are full of sentimental ads about motherhood, recounting all of the heartwarming reasons to thank moms. Of the list mentioned in saccharine terms, my mother did none. Not one story read. Not one boo-boo kissed. She had her own problems and I don't blame her.

Sometimes when I look in the mirror I see my mother's chin and it knocks me back a moment to see a part of her so plainly on my face. But then I tilt my head to the side and drop my nose. When I lean in close I recognize them: Mare eyes, soft and deep. They are the external marker of the change inside: I had gotten better at nurturing, better at saying no when I need to, and better at letting hard feelings go. I had become part of Windy's legacy, too and I hoped I was doing her proud

The Grandfather Horse

Spirit was my dream horse. The one I dreamed of before I was born and the one I pretended to be when I was a kid. The horse I held my breath and prayed for. He may well have existed without me, but I'm not sure I could ever have existed without him.

In the real world, my dream horse was not all that athletic. So there were injuries. It was no one's fault. He gloried in a powerful gallop, his hind legs churning soil up into the air in his wake. When he was seven, Spirit injured a tendon while playing in turn-out and two precious years were stolen as he recuperated on stall rest. He tried so hard for me, his heart took him farther than his body could go sometimes. When he retired ten years later with a second tendon injury, our riding days were over.

Retirement was Spirit's worst nightmare. He thought I had quit him. He didn't quit me, he never would, but now I was riding other horses but never him. He stood at the gate and slammed his bad leg against the metal rail each time I rode. For two years. Quitting was not in his playbook, he had no intention of giving up and it didn't matter how much it hurt his back and legs. He wanted our old spine-to-spine talks back. Sometimes I gave in and climbed on. He walked two or three steps and then stopped, his head drooped low. As I slid off, I told him how good he was. How beautiful his old sway back was to me. We spent years inside of each other's minds—it was a bittersweet habit now.

This midlife crisis of mine began the year my sweet friend

lost her fight with cancer. She was an artist and a lover of life. I remember the deep rust color of her hair and her squawk of a laugh. My friend fought the cancer with grace and courage, and when she finally entered the hospital for the last time, I spent bittersweet days there helping her ease away from her young life.

One afternoon I was alone with her for a couple of hours. Her husband had gone on a necessary errand and the sun was low in the sky; more friends would be there soon. She had a morphine drip to keep her comfortable as she dozed in and out of consciousness. She mumbled about bunnies and squirrels in her cup of ice chips, they alternately amused or worried her. I couldn't quite understand what she was saying but I hoped they looked like the ones in Disney cartoons.

Then her eyes opened in surprise and her voice was clear, "Spirit's here!" It was the last name I expected to hear. My Grandfather Horse, Spirit, was still young then, and although she'd scratched his nose once or twice, she was unfamiliar with horses and intimidated by their size. She would never climb on Spirit's back but now he was in her hospital room?

"What does he want?" I asked her, and after a pause to listen, she responded, "He wants to take me for a ride." I was a bit incredulous, but I said, "You should go!"

Her eyes fluttered closed, and I think she slept. Her body relaxed and her breathing settled to a softer rhythm. Her eyes were active under her eyelids, and dreaming peacefully, an hour passed. It was longer than she'd been able to rest recently. She woke, again with clear words, "We flew, he's so wonderful, we flew." I asked about it, but a nurse came in to check her vitals, and adjusted the morphine. Then her good husband returned and she drifted in and out. The moment was gone.

When I said good night, she said a few words that I didn't hear clearly, except for the word sister. I hoped she meant me but maybe she meant her and Spirit. My sweet friend passed a few hours later.

We should all have a horse called Spirit once. It names that ability horses have to travel between dreams and reality. But here at the hospital? Did some essence of him actually come? If it was her peaceful dream, why an animal she was afraid of? Did he come to let me know he was there to help? Or maybe it was just meaningless drug-induced chatter, but it cheers me up to think maybe, somehow, he carried her over some rough ground.

Almost ten winters had come and gone since then and my Grandfather Horse gets a little more transparent each year. He has no more trot left in him and he leaves his lunch unfinished to spend the warm hours napping on his nose. He finds a soft piece of dirt and grunts as he lies down. I wonder if he dreams as he gets closer to the edge. When he rests those old legs, where does his heart return to? Who comes to take him for a run?

Spirit's retirement was heartbreaking but still, we are partners. From breed shows to reining to dressage, from marriage to my work to the farm, he had always been family in my heart. How many times have I mucked his stall? Shared my watermelon? Altered my life for him? It was easy to get unstuck in time and travel back: I could close my eyes and I'd be on his back once more. Spirit was young, and we were galloping the old airstrip. As I leaned forward his mane blew across my face like a stream of cool water.

Spirit is a word synonymous with soul; it's no coincidence. He and I are part of an ancient tradition of horses and humans, and it was time to pay the tradition forward. Spirit watched over Clara the night she was born, and Lord knows, he had been watching over me forever. It's a bittersweet task, but I hope Spirit will stay and watch over Clara and me just a while longer. It would give us a leg up. We are better through his eyes.

And I hold strong for a time when Spirit and I will gallop together again, like prehistoric partners. For now, each day was one more chance to scratch those ears, clean the sleep-gunk out of his eyes and thank Spirit for sticking it out with me.

Dating my Own Species

Maned Sloth, Honey Badger, Spotted Moray, Black Rhinoceros, Scaly-tailed Possum, Giant California Sea Cucumber: They are all solitary animals that pretty much only get together to breed and raise young. Add my parents to the list. Okay, me, too. Only without the kid part.

It was surprising that I wanted to date at all. It wasn't like my experience with men was all that great growing up. After leaving home, I had been the survivor of some very unsavory dating interchanges. I chalked it up to instinct above common sense. Humans are herd animals, social just like horses and dogs. We are designed to date, even the introverted ones. Then on top of that, add the usual dose of cultural conditioning about marriage, but with my family's dysfunctional twist. It's the reason some of us leave home and make great life decisions, while others appear to have no sense at all.

In my youthful days, I mixed that with a fair amount of desperation and self-loathing. I'm not bragging, it was just in the bags I packed when I left home. Because I was introverted, I thought about it way too much. And then, being a herd animal, I got lonely. This is a wildly bad recipe for true love and harmony, but if I got bucked off, I climbed right back on.

And because the universe usually reflects back to us exactly what we ask for, the men I met were kind of like me, with other varied weirdness packed in their luggage from home. It felt familiar to meet someone with similar issues, almost like we were meant for each other. No blame, no regret. I did the best I could with the poor judgment I had because I wanted a relationship with someone of my own species.

Dating started to improve a bit in my twenties, once I had a dog. A dog regulated my coming and going in a more balanced way. There was someone else who had to eat and walk and sleep. Like a small furry anchor, a dog gave me someone to come home to. It encouraged me to try to make better dating choices, like I had something to lose. And when it didn't work out, and lots of times it didn't, I had my fur family on my side. Pathetic? Probably, but I didn't have many supportive humans to fall back on. I'm grateful to those dogs who slept close at night and got me out of the house during the day. When no one else did, they held the vision of me as lovable, lick-able, and even irresistible. I got stronger day by day, not because of family support or the love of a good man. I learned to love myself and make better choices because of my dogs' relentless unconditional love and acceptance, even when I did very little to deserve it. People never held that vision of me so true. There's an argument that twenty years of therapy helped, too.

Once horses were added to the mix, I got even better. Instead of wandering around parks and antique malls, I spent all my time at the barn. Like most horse-crazy girls, I learned compassion and communication from the horses there. Not everyone learns that at home, but if you don't learn it at the barn, you land on the ground a lot. When Spirit and I got together, I didn't know how to be a couple at first. It wasn't a perfect romance. There were years of missing the mark. We both had doubts but we didn't quit. We stayed together, even when it hurt. I turned out pretty okay. I have loved some good men and some men that didn't live up to the promise, but Spirit was constant. From a solid seat on his back, I could be my own boss mare.

The first few years on the farm, there was so much to do—so much adjustment—that I didn't make an effort to date. The horses were sound and I rode a lot. The llamas and I hiked in our spare time. After Spam died, Howdy, a new puppy, joined us. I managed to find a couple of new horse friends.

Eventually life got more or less settled and I got that old solitary-but-don't-wanna-be longing again. Sunday mornings were the most obvious time. I wanted to make pancakes. I wanted to lounge in bed and watch movies. Sometimes I even longed to converse in my own language.

So I went on a blind date. It wasn't really a blind date. He was the friend of a friend, and the party was already planned. My friend said he was really nice, he worked with her husband. She was concerned for my singleness, even a bit embarrassed by it. I met this woman through horses—she got hurt and I let her get her confidence back on one of my horses. She thought this blind date would return the favor.

The afternoon of the party I took a ride, mucked to clear my head, and then started the scrub. It had been a long time since my last date, so I took some safety precautions. I didn't shave my legs, I wore ancient cotton underwear. Simple enough, but just in case there was some unruly moment when my hormones betrayed my common sense, I wanted potential humiliation to weight the scales in a better direction. Amazingly, it did not always work. On the other hand, I applied a light coat of mascara. Full make-up for me, I felt like I had war paint on.

Now was when some women try dozens of outfits on, throwing them dramatically on the floor, one after another. Not me. I had a first date outfit. It really simplified things if I had the outfit all set up, kind of like people who had a funeral suit. I picked a garment in my favorite color, one that's multi-seasonal. I dressed for myself, meaning comfortable and soft. The neck opening was variable. I just want to say that men always know you have breasts, even in a turtle-neck. Even boys know it. Don't get me wrong, I'm not overly modest. I just owe it to all those suffragettes who fought their way out of corsets and into the voting booth. It's a shame that all these years later, women are still strapping themselves together in an effort to please a man who wears butt-crack jeans and horizontal-striped shirts that accentuate...never mind.

I looked great, like I worked in the sun all day and loved

it. I had my best accessory on all along: my teeth. Farm girls from the Midwest all have big teeth, with blinding smiles. It's my strong suit, unless I have a low-cut shirt on. Then my teeth don't matter at all.

My friend offered some advice to me, being an expert. She was currently married, which is apparently like a diploma from a trade school. She said, if I had to, absolutely had to, I could mention *a* horse and *a* dog. I should try to avoid talk of cats and at all costs, *never mention goats*. She seemed desperate for me.

I arrived at the party a bit late so I wouldn't be the first one there. I was still early, so I helped prep food in the kitchen and talked to a couple of really interesting women. I almost forgot that the party had a theme and it was me. I saw my friend make a frantic gesture as my date arrived. He was wearing a ratty T-shirt and old tennis shoes. I was pretty sure he knew his role, because it looked like he'd probably showered that morning. The good news was he didn't seem to be the sort of man who'd flinch at the sight of horse manure.

Eventually we met at the food table.

"Hi. How are you?" he asked. I'm sure I only imagined that the room hushed. We had small talk and artichoke dip, both nervous about failing our long-suffering host. Maybe he blinked one too many times when I told him I was an artist but he was okay.

The volume of the voices in the kitchen spiked and I peered over his shoulder. My friend was in a circle of people telling a story. The more they laughed, the louder my friend's voice became, until the laughter caught up again. My date stopped mid-sentence and turned to face the kitchen. Just then the story climaxed, she let out with a cackle and, "...two llamas in the kitchen, making tea!" The circle of onlookers threw back their heads, coughing with laughter, some doubled over. It didn't sound that funny to me.

At that moment, everyone in the kitchen turned toward us and fell silent. One or two women covered their mouths and dropped their eyes down to their shoes.

My date was about to continue what he was saying about his job, when my friend rushed over and apologized. She gushed, "I'm so sorry, I didn't think. It's embarrassing, such a faux-pas," she said. "It's all my fault." My date looked confused. I hadn't even admitted to having a dog yet and she was apologizing as if she had told him I'd done prison time for murder, drug smuggling, or shoplifting a sick kitten back in high school. Okay, guilty on that last count.

He was baffled, and he turned to me with furrowed brows. "I have llamas," I said. He waited. "Six llamas."

"Do you hike with them?" he asked, more curious than put off. "I see them on the trail all the time."

I never understand why we try to hide the inevitable. If my lifestyle was a deal breaker, did she think that if he proposed over the ham roll-ups and we married on the way home, it would be too late before he found out about the goats? I needed to reconsider this friendship.

My date said he would call.

After a few weeks I saw him again in a group of people. He stayed after the others had gone and apologized for not calling. "I've missed you," he said. "You've been on my mind. I meant to call. But I might be seeing someone."

"What does that mean?" I asked. He hemmed and thought, but he wasn't sure. "Would she mind if you kissed me?" I asked. He thought about it. "Probably yes," with a sly smile. It made sense now.

I ended the conversation. "Well then, it bothers me, probably yes, too." I had horses to feed.

A few months after that I decided to try online dating. I didn't have to, I always had the option of bar-hopping. But there was a change that happened to me when I walked into a bar. My voice went up a shrill three octaves and I squint my eyes all the time. If I just appeared a bit uncomfortable maybe I could pass, but instead I came off crazy and mean. Not to mention I was rarely conscious after nine p.m. It's a bizarre thing when online dating seems like the safe and sane alternative.

So I wrote out an ad. I used my usual approach; I told the truth. I tried to sound charming as I listed my real age. My real size. My real hobbies. I added a photo of me, with my big teeth smiling and my spikey white hair. It matched my beautiful Andalusian gelding, Nubè, standing right over my shoulder. It was truth in advertising—there was always a horse just over my shoulder.

I posted it online and within an hour a dentist emailed me. "You have a great smile," It was the first thing he said. I mean it—midwest farm teeth. We dated a while, he was edgy and romantic, hinting that he was going to move to the farm and build a new house after a few dates. It seemed a bit forward, but I listened because he said there would be a hot tub. Truly the state of bathtubs these days is dismal. He managed to hide his drug habit for almost three weeks, but I became suspicious. When I asked him about it, he informed me that his therapist recommended he not be in a relationship. I didn't argue the point.

Online dating was a crash course in finding out if I could take a sucker punch right in my self-esteem. Some people are brutally honest and some enjoy the game of deception. Some just choose the wrong words; communication is an art, after all. It took courage to put on that first date outfit week after week and admit to the world I was looking, and by definition, lacking. It is the ultimate strength to remain vulnerable; to keep a soft heart and ask the world for what I wanted. Cyberspace—I was learning to ride it.

I'd joined a local artist's co-op the previous year, and that summer, I volunteered my farm for the annual picnic. It was a fun day. Kids were playing soccer in the riding arena, being herded by a pack of dogs. The grill was hot, and everyone was sitting in the shade enjoying themselves.

I made runs to the kitchen, refilled drinks and brought the donkey and llamas out to meet and greet. As the party was winding down, I saw the co-op manager standing out in the barn. He had his nose lifted in the air like a big dog as he watched the sun head down toward Pike's Peak. He had been over there awhile so I went to ask if he wanted anything.

"Nope, I'm just fine," he said in a deep Texas accent. "I do love this farm." I believed him.

I worked in the co-op gallery every Friday. The classical music on the sound system always sounded like *muzak* to my ear so I brought music from home. The week after the party, I slipped in a Bob Wills and the Texas Playboys CD mid-morning. I didn't really think much about it, but the manager came barreling out of his office.

"Did you put this music on?" he asked, looking around to see who else was there. I smiled and nodded, not new to defending my musical tastes. "How do you even know about them?" Like you had to live in Texas to know the words to *San Antonio Rose*.

"Not only do I know who they are, I've ridden a musical dressage freestyle to the music of Bob Wills, Patsy Cline, and Roy Rogers, in costume, on my white horse." He gave a slight tilt to his head and squinted at me through bi-focals as if that would help make any more sense of me. "Aw-kay..."

We talked music and ordered take-out from the barbecue joint around the corner. The reason he acted like he owned Bob Wills was that he was related to one of the original Playboys. That counted as squatter's rights, at least. We became friends over shared music and Friday barbecue. I thought he was married.

Only he wasn't married and hadn't been for a while. I was out of the gossip loop because I was busy wearing my first date outfit threadbare. You can bet I grilled him about it. Then he asked me to dinner at my house. Why not? It wasn't like he hadn't met everyone out there already.

He arrived Saturday night, with a big pot of chili and a

guitar case. I valued our friendship. I wrestled with feelings of anticipation and dread. He pushed past me and made himself at home in the kitchen. When I offered him a beer he said, "No thanks, clean and sober for over a decade now. You go ahead, though," with such a relaxed confidence that I popped a bottle and watched him finish dinner. We made small talk until we sat down at the table and had (he was right to brag) spectacular chili; the old fashioned kind with nuance and spice. Dinner was perfect. He had my full attention.

For the last twenty years or so, I had been lying about cooking just to get out of it. I saw it as women's work that I did not enjoy. Like sewing and typing, cooking was one of those things I denied knowing, mainly for political reasons. I had long since learned that the one who did those things, didn't get to do other things. So I played possum.

Seeing a man in his full glory cooking and doing dishes can re-balance the universe a little bit. Then he suggested we go sit in the swing out by the pond, and he brought the guitar case along. I don't mean to sound cynical but I thought we might be pushing our luck. Dinner was so good. Why would he want to ruin it by singing? I was embarrassed already.

The last time a man sang to me was in high school. He sang Elton John's *Your Song*, but messed up the lyrics. There was a line about not remembering if her eyes were green or blue, but he sang black or blue. I bit my lip and practically had to choke myself.

I reluctantly dragged my feet out to the swing. The breeze ambled past; it was dusk and there were a couple of duck families taking in the air on the pond. He picked up the guitar and I held my breath, preparing to find kind excuses. But the notes were clear and sweet. His voice came in strong. He sang with confidence and quirkiness, and a dollop of big-dog Texas on top. He was fantastic. That was an understatement.

I think he planned the evening to show me who he was. He wasn't big on words, but I trust actions better anyway. A couple of hours passed, singing and laughing. The moon rose and I walked him to the driveway. He wrapped me in a hug and gave me a "Night, darlin'" and got in his car. Because when you've hit a home run and you know it, there's really no need to run the bases at breakneck speed. You can saunter your way to home plate, if you feel like it.

We didn't live happily ever after, but we did for a while. I loved his parents and we had a good life together. When we had parties, the men were in the kitchen and the women were in the barn. Sometimes he brought his guitar to the arena, and Spirit and I danced to his music.

But we got lazy and forgot to say thank you. We forgot what we had, and let the world make us less than we were. He left me on my birthday. The dogs missed him as much as I did. They would have looked at him with love still, but he was gone. The horses welcomed me in the barn. Their long necks encircled me, our hips and shoulders touched. They shared my breath until my heart rate calmed. Spirit was still there. And it wasn't my first rodeo.

Visitors by Bus

I was mailing a package at a shipping store, being half-mauled by a terrier while standing in line. He was jumping up on me and his owner was horrified. She apologized in a shocked tone, explaining that *her* dog never did that. In the dog's defense, I always had a very special stink to my feet. I carried with me a cornucopia of delightful smells from the several species in my barn. It drove city dogs nuts. My feet smelled like the exception to the rule, and it was enough to make a good dog go bad.

"*My* dog is a therapy dog," the woman said with pride that implied special consideration was required.

I smiled and said, "Yeah, they all are." But I offended her.

"*My* dog has a certificate."

I meant no disrespect. Hero and I were spending an evening a week visiting in a nursing home at the time. I was on her side. And there is no shortage of scientific proof that service dogs are capable of complex, near-magical tasks. Horses in therapeutic riding programs reduce handlers to goose bumps and tears routinely. And no matter how often we see it, humans are still in awe of an animal's power to pry our hearts open.

I was born with a full set of senses but lost some along the way. Some of my hearing was the first to go, thanks to a series of childhood ear infections. My sense of smell was limited after a broken nose which was the result of a run-in with a cross-eyed Suffolk ram when I was in second grade. Not having a sense of smell in the barn isn't the worst affliction. I've always been far-sighted but if I triangulate llama gazes, or follow donkey ears, I see all kinds of visitors that my human eyes would have missed. I've depended on animals for help with other senses as well: like a sense of confidence and safety. Some of us find a sense of belonging with animals that we don't find as sweet anywhere else. And animals don't discriminate on grounds of disability, mental or physical. They help us all equally whether we think we need therapy or not.

By the fifth year, we were fully settled residents in the area and more visitors came to the farm. Sometimes it was someone who arrived with their arms and hearts wide open, so ready to hand off their burden and sometimes it was the last person you would suspect, someone so shut down that their eyes were flat. But a dog would take them in hand, or sometimes a goat. Cats heeded the call if necessary and they weren't busy killing rodents at the time.

If the horses got involved everyone was lifted to a higher place. They have that ability. I never fully understood how, but sullen teenagers got child-like and laughed out loud. Elders glowed as they were reminded of animals they missed from the past. Always there was a range of warm emotions, followed by quiet reflection.

During that time I was doing home health care for the friend of a friend. I sometimes drove my client to appointments and shopping and one day she asked if we could stop at a nursing home so she could visit a friend. We walked into the greeting area and there was a large aviary of finches. The hallway was busy, every door decorated with names and photographs. It reminded me of the place Hero and I had gone for visits but most of the patients here were younger than I expected, or at least not elderly. The staff was working for a homey atmosphere but it was still a little sad there. I chatted with people in the hallway while my client visited her friend. The social worker came through doing rounds and my client introduced us and then blurted out that they should all come out to my farm. My client had never been out to my farm but she insisted it would be great. The social worker's eyes lit up—she was always looking for outings. I said yes without really thinking what I was agreeing to. The social worker and I exchanged emails; still, I had no doubts at all until the bus pulled in. Who gets company in a bus?

I had thought it would be the usual stroll through the pens, but two people were in wheel chairs and the ones who were able to walk were not all that steady. So I hunted down enough lawn chairs and eventually everyone was settled in a line. There were three men and six women, plus the social worker. They were quiet, and a couple of the women looked nervous. I'm not sure they were animal lovers, maybe they just wanted out for the day. All the men looked bored. As for me, I still hadn't thought this out.

I went and got Ernest. It was a trade-off. Donkeys can be skittish with unfamiliar people, but they were also short and less intimidating than the horses or llamas for people sitting in chairs. I brought Ernest out on a long lead and hoped he'd know what to do. We started at one end of the line, and he gently stepped forward and put his head in a touchable position. He stood still, and made eye contact. The first woman in the line was shy and reluctant to reach out. He lifted his ears toward her and she smiled. Everyone in the line watched them, and finally Ernest pushed his nose out an extra inch and she responded with a light touch. When she was ready, he moved to the next person in line. If a scratch was offered he politely accepted, even on his ears. I kept a look-out to make sure everyone was safe, that Ernest was okay, and gave a bit of history on donkeys.

Half-way down the line sat a very tiny woman, so pale that she was almost transparent. When Ernest got to her, she let out a loud shriek. She had a tight, erratic body movement. It might have just been a release of energy. Everyone startled but Ernest. He got even more quiet, and while others laughed and caught their breath, the tiny woman started to reach out. Her arthritic hand bounced and jerked, she gritted her teeth with effort.

Everyone was quiet now, watching her reach. We all thought if she got close she would probably thump him or poke him in his eye. But Ernest was steady and she was determined. Finally she made contact, her little fist of fingers right in the middle of his forehead, fluttered like a bird. He didn't blink an eye and she exhaled a shallow breath. Her hand steadied and Ernest wiggled his lips and showed a bit of tooth. Smile enough. She slumped back in her chair and everyone laughed and congratulated her. As he continued to slowly move along the line, each person did something slightly different, and Ernest responded individually. Ernest, the abused donkey from the auction, welcomed our guests with grace.

The last man in the line wore a plaid flannel shirt and a scowl. He looked grouchy and bored, and the others seemed anxious about him in some way. He kept his eyes low and didn't say much, but there was tension. Ernest came to him and dropped his head lower almost offering his forehead. The old man was still and Ernest waited. Time ticked by and I almost led Ernest away. At the last moment, Ernest took another step closer. The man gave in and lifted his hand. He didn't pet Ernest, he just laid his hand on him and held it there for a long moment. This grouchy man fumbled for a moment and brought a peanut out of his pocket and offered it to Ernest. Ernest politely took the peanut and chewed it. The grouch cracked the faintest smile. Ernest turned and we went back to the barn.

Next I brought out Spirit. We approached the line of visitors and he was curious as he dropped his head low into the first lap. By now the people were more comfortable and chatting between themselves a bit. Spirit is a large horse and from their angle sitting in a chair, he was tall enough to block out the daylight. But without direction, just like Ernest, he slowly went from person to person. Slow and sweet, Spirit lowered his head to each person, as they asked. Spirit could be a real handful riding, depending on who you were. He was gentle with kids but he was an emotional horse with that innate tendency to reflect back what he felt. He always pointed out angry people to me, so I worried maybe this group would confuse him. Spirit moved down the line and seemed to especially enjoy the women cooing over him. He responded a bit differently to each person and again, each person felt that their acknowledgment from him was special. And it was. Finally the end of the row peanut test and again, the peanut was received gently. The grouch gave a little sigh.

I always had the same feeling at a time like this—whether it was my dog Hero at the nursing home, or this day—that I don't really control my animals. Whatever they do is honest. They understand compassion. When they are in this kind of situation, I have learned to trust them. To hold my tongue and just watch. They always comprehend the situation and usually understand more than I know.

Time for the llamas next. I brought the two boys, Sebastian and Holiday, out on leads. These sweet boys, so curious and so gentle, went down the line slow and calm. No one had seen a llama close before and these were very close. They lowered their long necks so their noses were an inch away from that person's nose and gently smelled each person's breath. People spoke quietly to them and they seemed to agree.

The llamas looked kind of magical, almost unicorn-like, even to my eye. The group was mesmerized. Down the line of visitors we went again and once more the animals had some kind of unique acknowledgment for each person, from both llamas at once, each person doubly acknowledged. Finally, came the peanut test. This time the peanuts were taken and the grouch let out a cough/laugh when he saw their gums. Llamas have a separation in their upper lip and no front teeth on their upper gum. This group of people was a bit dentally challenged, so the llamas were a special hit. Chowing down on the peanuts was the very best and as the grouch chuckled, it allowed everyone else to laugh. Maybe the grouch was the alpha mare in the group.

What did I have to lose? The animals all looked like world

class therapy animals, the kind with *certificates*, so I got the goats out. That was wild and fool-hardy. The last time they got out when company was here, they jumped on top the picnic table and ravaged the melon salad. Goats are free thinkers and none of the rules apply. Even gravity rarely works on them. It's a bit like turning a biker gang loose, but this day they walked slowly and did just what the rest did, starting at the same end and walking along. Why did all the animals treat this group like a receiving line at church? On they went, getting scratches, keeping all four feet miraculously on the ground without crunching toes with their pointy little hooves. Of course they nibbled on the occasional shoe lace or shirt cuff, which caused uproarious laughter. The most unpredictable of my animals appeared to be doing golden retriever impressions. I half expected to see a herd of pigs fly over.

By now everyone watched the final peanut moment. I'm not sure the grouch brought the peanuts for that purpose, but it had become the final test. Peanuts were odd snacks for the horses, but since goats eat cardboard and tin cans, they thought it was a delicacy. I don't give treats often and sometimes animals can be food aggressive. That day every animal was delicate about taking a peanut, one at a time, from the old grouch. And all the humans waited for the peanut response at the end of the line. The goats got congratulated, and everyone chuckled. The older women who were timid were now audible in their enthusiasm and the grouch had become a revered and charming leader.

I thought we were about done, so the next request surprised me. They asked to see me ride. It had come up in small talk that I did dressage and now they asked to see some. I hadn't considered riding. These folks were so physically limited that I thought it would be almost unkind. I could be small-minded that way. I agreed and Ernest came back out to chat with the people when I tacked up my horse. Dodger was the athletic wild child, too hot to be patient with novice riders and certainly too hot for these visitors.

It was about two hundred yards from where everyone was sitting out to the riding arena; much too far for this group to manage on uneven ground. So they turned their chairs a little and we came to them. That was challenging enough; Dodger and I only had a small piece of hard ground to work on. Jeans and tennis shoes aren't the approved apparel for Dressage, but I grabbed my helmet and mounted. I felt Dodger swell underneath me, he was ready. I asked for a bit of a slow trot and felt each stride as his shoulder reached out in front of us. Dodger was a proud horse, a fine trait in a dressage mount. He arched his neck, collected into the small space and somehow inflated himself at the same time. He wanted to show off. For this crowd? We did shoulder-in and extensions at the trot. With just a few strides to show in the small space, we had to be quick and immediately responsive to each other. We cantered, almost on the spot, a pirouette, a half pass, flying changes every few strides. We did all the movements of upper level work we knew. We did them in a tiny space and for a moment, we lost ourselves in the work. This crowd of folks who knew nothing about riding were silent. By the time I noticed how quiet they were, I feared that we had bored or offended them. We halted solid and square, I released the reins, and Dodger dropped his head. They were holding their breath. Had I done something wrong? Then I saw the tiny woman had tears streaming down her face. The social worker started clapping and everyone joined in.

"More!" she called. I always have a secret dream of being asked to ride. I know my horse passion and the long hours of training don't mean much to most people; it can be hard to understand the finesse involved. I never ask people to watch my passion. When Dodger and I stopped again, I was beaming. As I rode, my default smile was so big that my teeth got dry and my lip stuck to my gums.

The louder they cheered, the more Dodger did. He was dynamic and powerful, all the movements done with hot energy and cool control. The lighter I asked the more he offered. I fell in love with him all over again, for the millionth time.

Then Dodger pulled the bit from my hands and marched to the first person in our farm receiving line. He dropped his proud, aristocratic head, slowly and with great dignity, to each person in the line. The women were especially awestruck. Dodger seemed like a valiant knight to me sometimes—did they see him that way too? His beauty could be almost foreboding, but today it was a special gift to those whose movement was slow and painful. He gave them wings and they all loved him; his quietness after the dance was so inclusive, so encompassing. Finally, with such respect, such reserve, he deigned to accept a peanut.

By now hours had passed but as late as our guests were, the leaving was slow. I helped them back into the bus; each one slowed by their exhaustion, and me, overwhelmed by their gratitude. The grouch actually hugged me! The world was lighter that day. No one was thinking what had been lost or what was to come, only that they were lighter. There was chatter and giggling back and forth among the formerly silent group. The social worker's hug was bone-crushing as she thanked me again and again. Ernest and I waved as they drove off.

I did nothing at all. It was all the animals. I was proud of each of them. My very best days are when others get to see them as I do. Most folks tell me what hard work it is, how expensive they must be, and how sad it is to lose them. All good reasons to not have animals. To ride the quicksilver magic of animals involves shutting up and opening to possibility past our own mental limitations. We have to let them be magic—it's who they all are, if we get our egos out of the way.

Some days I wondered if choosing to live with the population of a small zoo would seem to imply a greater need for therapy than the average person. Maybe I was crazy enough to need a whole staff of therapists. Or maybe a large animal family is just a sure sign of extreme and abundant mental health.

The next morning I was in the shower planning ways to do

more farm visits when I noticed a giant rectangular hole in the ground just outside the window. I put a bathrobe on and the dogs and I went out to investigate. The dogs skidded to the edge, front paws teetering. So that's where my septic tank was, exactly. The cement lid collapsed inside; the view was ugly. No more ranch guests until I got that figured out, but on the bright side, no dogs had fallen in.

Parting Ways With Dodger

We'd been on the farm for seven years when Dodger dumped me. Better said, we parted ways. We were playing with another trainer and her horse in the arena, in that way that we never let our clients see. It was a made-up game that was a cross between tag, cutting each other like cattle, and bumper cars. The horses taught us how to play. There were lots of laughing screams and happy ears. Then it happened, my fault entirely. I went one way and Dodger went the other. It was silly but in an instant I was on my back in the dirt. He was seventeen years old and it was our very first unplanned dismount. The best part happened after I hit the ground.

Just like any wreck, time moved in ultra-slow motion. I hit hard and my helmet took the impact. Dodger's belly was still in the air right above me. He blocked out the sun and I immediately knew that he would step on me. There was no way to avoid it, one of his hooves had to land on my torso. It was going to hurt. Then at the last fraction of a second, he twisted his body into an impossible kink and his hind end flung to the side like the crack of a whip. His hooves met the earth with one of them landing on the hem of my T-shirt. Not me, just the T shirt. His front legs were on one side of me and the back legs on the other. He had practically ruptured vertebrae trying to avoid stepping on me. It wasn't a trick you could train. This position in the dirt with my horse straddling me was a position I had earned—not an accident. We both knew he missed me on purpose. Then he curved his neck and dropped his head down to the ground to look me in the face.

In that instant when he was still in the air, I saw both our lives pass before my eyes. From before we had spooked at our own shadows, to years of dressage success, to chasing rabbits on our farm—all of my very finest moments. He taught me to stand tall, to live with integrity, to know that I was good enough. Some days I still lie in his shadow.

I lost Dodger much too young. He died of colic that next autumn.

A storm was coming in; black clouds and howling wind. The temperature had dropped twenty degrees by early afternoon. He started to look just a bit off. He barely wanted to eat and his flank was tense. The symptoms weren't dramatic but I knew every nuance of his body. We moved quickly, not taking any chances. Rather than call a vet out, I hauled him to the clinic.

There were already two other horses there with similar symptoms. Between the extreme weather change, their delicate digestive system, and a hundred other variables, it's unpredictable. Still, after decades of research and so much improvement in technology, colic remains the number one killer of horses. Even with all the veterinary skill in the world, treating it is an art that still seems to rely on luck as much as anything. It isn't fair.

By the time we got to the clinic, Dodger's pain was visible in his eyes and his breathing. He had no gut sounds, his bowels weren't moving. As usual, he stood proud. The vet did all the right tests and procedures, but as the evening dragged on, Dodger remained stoic. I knew it would resolve any moment and we would all be relieved. He was filled with drugs but the pain continued. His eyes were calm, even elegant.

Then close to midnight, while the vet was gone running a blood test in the lab, Dodger's eyes changed. I knew immediately that he had taken a turn. I called the vet in and he saw it too and checked his vitals one more time. The numbers were all bad. The vet had been fighting hard for all the horses there, he didn't want to see it any more than I did, but Dodger was failing fast and we had no choice. Brutal as it was, we needed to euthanize him and there was no room inside the clinic. We had to take him outside. It wasn't that I was capable of doing any of this—I pretended to be strong for him. I did what had to be done.

The blizzard was pushing hard with cutting temperatures and horizontal snow. I led Dodger outside; his steps were uneven as he wobbled in the wind. "Good boy, my perfect boy." The vet and vet tech were in front of us cutting a path through the snow. We made it to a spot behind the clinic, just barely out of the wind. While the vet tech held a flashlight, I kept a quiet hand on Dodger's neck and praised him again and again, "My best boy," as they prepared the two shots. Dodger was shivering with pain and confusion, unsteady on his feet.

I don't blame my vet for what happened next. It's not always controllable, even in the best of conditions. The first shot went in Dodger's vein, and in the process of changing syringes, the needle came out. The flashlight found the needle in the snow and the vet had to find the vein again before giving the second shot. Dodger fell half way to the ground and I hit my knees, holding his head up for the vet. The last word Dodger heard me say was, "Hurry!"

Just like any wreck, time moved in ultra-slow motion. My heart stopped with his. This time it was me hovering in the air over him. I didn't want to let it end. I saw my life without him, knocked to the ground. It felt like a giant hoof crushed my heart. I knew what death meant—it was permanent. There would be no do-overs. When time started again, he was gone.

That was our finish. It was a cold, painful passing; he deserved better. I gasped for air to fill the void inside and then let out a gut-splitting howl that the wind took away as soon as it left my lips.

Back inside the clinic, the vet worked with the other horses. I signed paperwork and tried to keep my mind steady. The vet tech came back in to give me a bag with Dodger's beautiful tail in it. Does that sound ghoulish? It was a gift of respect, a small apology. We remember horses by weaving their hair into bracelets. It was what she could give me.

The road home was covered with white, tunneled over by dark sky. My headlights cut through the sideways snow but I still saw nothing but tears and windshield wipers. The truck and hollow trailer slowly found the way to our home farm. How could I leave him there? The house was cold and the dogs were quiet. I knew his body was covered with snow by now. I was greeted by the oil portrait that Dodger proudly posed for a few years earlier that hung over my dining room table. His beauty cut sharply against my last moments with him. Would I ever know such wholeness again? I felt horrible guilt as the last moments replayed in my mind again and again. I lost him again and again. I would have done anything to spare him such an ugly death. Even then I knew Dodger would never hold a grudge. This last indignity did not diminish him, and this one day could not negate all that came before. Dodger was a credit to his ancestors in life and in death. Me, not so much.

I lost a few friends in the months that followed, the people who had liked him more than me. Dodger had a way of inspiring riders that felt like enlightenment and our farm was so much drabber without him. Or maybe it was like parents who look at each other with nothing in common after the kids leave home, realizing that sharing a love of someone is not the same as loving each other. I could understand that. We just mourned him.

I'm haunted by Dodger still. Sometimes I see him out of the corner of my eye, grazing beside the arena as I'm training. Sometimes while I'm on another horse I feel a spark of Dodger's brilliance and his memory gallops back. The loss is bittersweet forever.

Maybe it would be easier to just stop riding. Is it cruel to always be aware that the horse I'm on falls short? It isn't that I can't get over Dodger, it's that his standard became mine. It isn't fair to judge another horse against him. Dodger was larger than life, but life without him continued. So I still ride, waiting for a moment, just a stride or a transition, that reminds me of him. Then I squeeze myself into that tiny place and breathe it large, so that I can bask there and remember what it felt like to be lifted and held by Dodger, just one more time. I still ride. He might come back to me some place I don't expect. I still ride. I can't stop.

And in that particular kind of weather when clouds move low and fast, the wind howls around corners, and the temperature plummets, the horses become as unsettled as the atmosphere. Spring and fall bring this kind of barometer-bouncing weather. There is a name for it, but I don't like to say it out loud. Colic weather. It's horrible luck. But when I feel it in my bones, I spend extra care. I put out too much hay for the cold night and check for evidence of the full range of bodily functions. Cohabiting with colic is part of the price of admission to any barn and as I finish the night check, I remember all the good horses gone too soon. They are still part of my herd.

Awe is the word that best describes what I feel about horses. Awe is defined in the dictionary as a mixed emotion of reverence, dread, and wonder inspired by authority, genius, or great beauty. It is a perfect description. In spite of spending hours every day with horses, I am constantly awe-struck by them; spell-bound by their intellect and humor, by their strength and physicality, by their breath on my cheek.

Part of the awe of horses is their fragility also. From their first steps on wobbly knees to the geriatric years of sway-backs and useless teeth, every day we have with them is a kind of victory over the impossibility of their strength and imperfection. To share your life with a horse means opening your heart wide enough for big hooves to clomp around inside, staying vulnerable enough to understand him, and yet strong enough to survive him. When Dodger died, the hole left behind eclipsed the world for a while, until the memory of that heart-felt awe overcame the loss. If the beauty of a horse is the sum of his bravery and vulnerability, then maybe that beauty is what we hope to emulate.

Bird-watching is for Eggheads

My pond, my pond: It was love at first sight. A water attraction was a cure for the flat, windy visual drought on the farm. My pond is one of a series of marshes, tiny streams, and ponds that wander across the prairie. There's a bit of a valley that crosses my farm, not much—this is the prairie after all—but the downslope that gave us a small break from the wind, and also let water gather in a pool here for a while before it continued south. Each day the sun set over my pond with Pikes Peak as a backdrop. The view was more than enough but the pond brought a world of its own that I hadn't expected. It was the farm equivalent of an office water cooler and bird-of-the-month wall calendar all in one. After years of being stuck on the freeway listening to traffic reports in Denver, the pond gave me a different kind of traffic report. The kind of traffic that enriched each day.

I used to be the sort of person who thought bird-watching was for eggheads. For people who didn't have dogs or horses. People who liked life a little distant and impersonal. I want to be very clear: It isn't just that I was wrong. I was blind. I was stupid.

Just after moving to the farm, I bought a log swing to sit on while pondering the pond. I envisioned myself reclining on designer pillows, sipping Chardonnay with classic literature in my lap. I had this romantic notion that I'd have time for beach behavior. I was as wrong about that as I was about bird-watching. Wherever I was, my eyes pulled to the pond. It was a dependable destination, not prone to superficial deception. If there was a warm day in February that previewed spring a few weeks early, the pond ice held firm to the season and told the truth, without a trace of spring fever or wishful thinking.

In the dark months of winter, the pond froze over gray and flat. Sometimes there were lonely paw prints on the ice but no birds. Every non-color on the prairie seemed the very definition of the dead of winter. It was a monotone landscape with not many trees to distract my sullen gaze from acres of dried prairie grass and hard ground. In town there was visual relief from the monotony; shapes of buildings broke up space and landscaping created texture. There was color on billboards and cars. Here on the prairie the plain, dead of winter truth was unavoidable.

And just when three layers of clothing felt like enough, the wind kicked in like a boat load of drunken pirates, cursing and careening across the farm, blowing away any hope the precipitation had given for a green spring. The wind left a moon-scape desert, frozen and parched, as our snow was making somebody else's pasture green. It made us all itchy.

In protected sides of barns, stalls and corners, small brown sparrows got out of the wind. They hopped up like dust-bunnies when interrupted from hay seeds and stolen duck chow. They hunkered down and flew low, and shared my opinions on an early spring. Tiny little lives maybe but we shared a home.

In the winter the sun was out and the sky was blue, but the sun's heating element didn't seem to work. Looking out the window, it looked just like any summer day except the ground was dead-tan and it was two degrees outside. The horses conserved energy and warmth with a blunt refusal at turnout time. "No, thanks. I'm fine right here." Instead they stood in their runs out of the wind and soaked up whatever the sun was giving out.

Shiny black grackles roosted along the backs of the horses, from right between the horse's ears all the way to the top of their tails, as many as seven or eight grackles per horse. They cackled in an abrasive East Coast accent and left droppings in manes and tails. The horses didn't mind their company. In the winter, grackles get a white fleck to their feathers. I knew this because I broke down and bought a field guide to birds. That's how bad it got. Now here I am, writing a field guide to my farm.

Every January I started looking for a sign. It was way too early for a hint of spring, but too cold for much else outside. The days had begun to lengthen, just a minute at a time. The ducks waddled out to the pond to check for a thaw now and then, but then returned to their half-frozen, duck-sized water tub. There was no joy.

Then one day, usually in late February, the sun felt warm on my skin, the one square inch that was uncovered. Temps weren't above freezing, but it had been so long since the sun gave up a degree more than daylight, that any heat was noticeable. Instantly, every animal was flat on the ground like oiled-up sunbathers at the pool, soaking up the marginal warmth.

The next week the temperature shot all the way up to 37 degrees. Mourning doves were the first birds to return, cooing a bird purr. The sound made it feel warmer. They marched around on the ground pecking at dirt to let me know that life down there might still exist. Most of the Canada geese still flew over at altitude. The ponds were still closed for the season.

Then one not-quite freezing morning in April, the Grandfather Horse managed a breakout. Some foolish human left a gate open, like every year, accidentally on purpose. It was literally heart-stopping to watch a dead-lame elderly horse lift himself up for his Annual Spring Canter. Would his legs hold him? The others followed, running on tippy-toes with flagged tails. It didn't last long and the Grandfather led them all back into their pen for water soon enough. Still, his crime spree was an undeniable rite of spring, along with the joint-aching hangover the next day. The first sweat of spring on a horse had a particular odor that make the grackles really happy and the roosting number doubled per horse.

The Annual Spring Canter means we survived winter. Let the frozen hose flow again and give me back that hour of light, it's spring! The pond stayed conservative with just a few inches melted around the edge but in one spot, it became the size of the domestic duck's wading pool. The wild birds arrived immediately, like an oasis in a desert. Canada geese flew in so low that the sound of their wings was audible. Then it was flaps down and webs wide as they skated across the ice, until they stopped or tumbled into the water at the end of the skid. The sheet of ice on the pond got a bit smaller every day in direct proportion to the abundance of honking and quacking.

The mountain bluebirds dropped by the farm just after the mourning doves and the robins. They had a frosty blue color just a slight tone off from sky blue. If enough of them were in the air, they made air look thicker, almost like water. It was a bird optical illusion. One arrived and then another; some years it was a few hundred and some years the sky was saturated. They met on the prairie and when they reached some sort of critical mass, they all turned on a wing and headed to the mountains for the summer. Gone in a blink, like ice in the sun. They go some other direction in the fall when they leave the mountains. It's a one-way ticket from our prairie.

On the pond, pairs of mallards talked too loud, quacking it up to impress everyone. When it got quiet I knew the girls were hatching eggs. Sometimes my pond was surveyed by a mated pair of Canada geese. Like a real estate agent, I tried to convince them that my pond had all the conveniences and was the perfect place to raise a family. They marched around and honked about it. They checked the wind and the food supply, and then moved on. I am not sure how we failed the geese, but they chose a better neighborhood at the pond a quarter-mile down the road.

Ducks are much less concerned about the details, and in the course of spring and summer, I had a half dozen broods of ducklings born. When they first began to swim with their moms, they were so tiny and round that they looked like little pebbles skittering across the water. The ducklings grew larger, but diminished in numbers daily. I didn't usually see the killing, but the attrition was visible. Same with the baby bunnies and rodents. Infant mortality was very high around the pond. They were a notch in the circle of life. I might not like it but it was undeniable, even dependable. Even tiny brief lives were part of the plan.

The horses were in full shed now, blowing out their frayed winter coats. It was as big an event as the pond melt. Horses lose all their hair twice a year, as new hair grows to take its place. Spring was the season to itch; pairs of horses stood grooming each other, leaving teeth marks and clumps of hair in the ground. Some horses just roll on the ground hard enough to leave a hair outline like crime scene tape. I hung a shedding blade on my muck cart so I could join in. A few kinds of birds swooped in and carried away a beak-full of hair for nest padding. Horse hair mixed with mud made brick-hard barn swallow nests that stuck to the barn rafters for years.

Barn swallows were just a bit more elite than the little sparrows of winter. They wore a sophisticated peach-colored vest under a midnight blue suit and had an exaggerated cut to their wings. They did aerobatics like tiny fighter jets. But when it came to parenting, they had the diligence of a vulture! The couple worked together to build the nest and then one sat on the eggs while the other hunted. Because they were wild animals who chose to live with domesticated ones, we all watched the daily drama unfold. Once the eggs hatched, the tag-team baby care began. That was the scary job, those massive yellow would-be-beaks opened way too wide and the shrill screams—they were baby bird monsters! While one parent found an endless supply of bugs to fill those gaping beaks, the other did home security and dive bombed anyone who appeared to be a threat. They were fearless against all comers when it came to protecting the babies. Each time I came to the barn, I got the air attack. Then the parents shifted weight on their tiny feet on a fence panel under their nest and glared at me until I left. I loved the audacity of these birds.

Hank the barn cat may have been a fair fight with Half-Tail, the coyote, but these barn swallows totally intimidated him. He couldn't get within twenty yards of the barn. Sometimes I kept him in the house just so I didn't have to watch the humiliation. What would it have been like to be raised by such fiercely protective parents? I especially envied the baby swallows once it was time to leave the nest. They all seemed especially frail when they glided out for the first few flights with parents shadowing babies like a fighter escort squadron. Somehow they all managed to get to the round pen. Mine had fence panels that were narrow pipes, so it was a good roost. They perched facing each other and practiced their swoop and land technique from one side of the circle to the other. At the end of the day, they flew back through the barn door and into the nest. Each day they ventured farther, till they were dive bombing the pond. Then they were gone and the parents started over again in their empty nest.

Some of the birds who visited us were memorable individuals. More than once there have been lost loons who have gotten blown to the ground during a storm. We don't have loons in Colorado, so there is no telling how far off course he was blown, but a loon needs water to take off. He can't actually walk on land. It was like a carnival game to toss a blanket over his pointy sharp beak weaving back and forth and even then he pecked an attack at me for trying to move him. I was nearly as afraid as he was that my attempted rescue would kill him but eventually we made it out to the pond. He spent a day there getting his bearings and then he was gone. I have no doubt he found his way home.

By late spring, the herons were back. Great white herons and blue herons glided onto the pond like pterodactyls, legs tucked up tight and neck angled in. After the stretched-out bodies of ducks and geese in flight, these gliding origami herons seem otherworldly. They stalked the edges of the pond balanced on bony knees, they wandered in the pasture extending long necks all the way to the ground. Herons were all stiff and flexible at the same time. Best of all, they perched in trees. How was that possible? Long branch-like legs holding onto—branches. Usually singletons, and often more shy than other birds, the grace of these birds was ethereal and prehistoric all at once. Have you ever heard a heron? Their voice is the price they pay for their elongated grace. A hoarse grating squawk, a couple of octaves lower than would be polite, came choking out of that long neck. Probably a small price to pay for so much physical beauty.

As weeks pass, the bird traffic came and went. Some traveled in big flocks, like the yellow-headed blackbirds who filled entire pens looking for leftovers. They turned in unison when taking off and went from black to a rich ocher yellow in the flip of a wing. Great-tailed grackles had a long graceful tail, truth in advertising, that was vertical and as stylized as a sumi brush painting, but they are loud. Hundreds settled into the tree by the barn each morning and chattered up such a racket that sometimes I tossed a pebble to make them fly away and give me a peaceful muck. It never worked. If I managed to hit the tree, none went very far and they somehow got even louder.

Meadowlarks were my favorite song bird; it was a bright whistle sort of trill that sounded like a synonym to *country* in my ear. I usually heard them more than saw them, but one year a meadowlark shadowed me most all summer while I was mucking. I called him Peg. Like Half-Tail the coyote, he had a distinctive physical appearance, a full leg but no foot on the end. He followed me from pen to pen, pegging along singing and snacking. He stayed within ten feet of me and the muck cart, so much closer than other birds. We were friends. He was gone in the fall, but the next summer he returned. If I had known he would become a perennial visitor, I would have given him a more flattering name. By the third year, I was doing some training at a neighboring barn, and he showed up there and followed me for the next two years at both barns. If I rode, he came out by the arena. Was he just that social? The donkey chased him some but he stayed true. Another year of mucking together and that was all. I suppose he was old, or maybe he retired in a warmer climate, but I noticed his little self missing, and mourned him.

He had been a good companion.

I wondered how many of the other birds were familiar old friends but without the marks to show me. Did they return to my farm for some sweet reason? Did they consider us that inter-species side of the family in Colorado?

Many of the birds, like Peg and the barn swallows, were bright colored jewels that flashed in shadows: Bright red finches, emerald hummingbirds or screaming blue jays. Some were remarkable for their size. The first time I saw a great horned owl, it was the middle of the night. I got up for a drink and saw him when I checked the horse pen. He looked like a piece of fire-wood balanced on the fence, twenty feet from my window. I couldn't make him out, such an odd shape. Then he turned toward me and I saw his feather horns. At first he didn't look like a bird because he had no neck, and in that second, he spread his massive wings and lifted efficiently into the air. Gone in an instant and I wanted to see him again. Then two years later, in the first week of August, three great horned owls played a marathon dating game by the pond. By the end of the squawking and flapping month, I didn't miss them at all.

Sometime around Labor Day, like a shift change at a factory, all the ducks and herons were gone and that same day the hawks returned. Prairies were made for hawks. Their particular voice floats in just the same way that they hang in mid-air, looking side to side for prey. Hawks seem like loners, even when small birds flew along. Hawks sang the song of the prairie with dry-throated love.

When the goats were young, they followed me all day while I worked, so it was natural to celebrate Happy Hour with them. I got a beer from the fridge and leaned against the small barn. The goatees sat on my lap and looked for trouble. They nibbled buttons and checked my hair for carrots until they finally settled into an ear scratch. Meanwhile, I checked my mental list: One job finished, sip and breathe, three more added. A longer sip with eyes closed while the tiny bones in my feet complained.

One early fall day, a shadow passed over, large enough that I felt darkness and shade over my body through my eyelids, large enough that the goats stopped chewing their cud and looked up. I squinted in the afternoon sun, no noise, a glider maybe? No, it had wings.

Every now and then, I saw a big hawk and wondered if it was an eagle. Hawks are big, owl wing spans are amazing, but this bird dwarfed all the others. His shadow covered us again, he soared in a circle, low and slow. Taking time for eye contact with a tilt of his head, my chin dropped open; he was huge. Again, he passed over and his lazy shadow rolled along behind. He made eye contact with each pass.

The llamas and horses stopped eating, all eyes and ears stretched forward. Then Sebastian, the llama, let his nose follow the bird, then his legs. He followed on a large lazy circle, cantering at gliding speed, escorting the eagle from the ground below. It was a golden eagle; I didn't need my field guide for this guy. I did look up his wing span later: seven feet! No wonder. His circles soared wider and wider, but each lap he sailed back close to me and gave a passing nod as his shadow covered us. The circles grew larger and took in the whole south pasture, as Sebastian continued to trace his path on the ground and the whole herd watched. Time slowed, but he never extended past our fence line. When the eagle's reconnaissance mission was through, he took one last low pass over me and seemed to hang still in the air a final moment. Then he straightened from his circle and flapped twice. He was immediately up and gone. I felt the rush of air from his wings as Sebastian came to a stop next to us. All eyes watched the eagle soar into the sunset. For a moment or two, there was a respectful silence, then the horses resumed their dinner, the goats went back to chewing my hair, and I drained the last of my beer, thankful for a big brother llama who watched for strangers.

Now it was full-on autumn. The sunrise was later and slower, but the pink and gold colors seemed worth the wait. Tomato plants had wilted black, but the trees had frosted and toasted to richness. I heard big weather was coming next week. Those were precious days.

Groups of Canada geese were back, another sure sign of change. Some lay over on the pond and rested a day or two on the way to warmer places. Those visitors might be my all-time favorites. I watched them on the farm on Leaf River as a kid. You could question the morals of herons or great horned owls, but never Canada geese. They mate for life, and travel in a flock. Horse-people call that a herd.

Each time a flying "V" formation went over, I paused and watched with some respect. They helped each other. Bird-dork that I had become, I looked it up. With each flap of the wing, *uplift* was created for the birds that followed. Flying in this way, the flock had a 71% greater flying range than if each bird flew alone. I looked it up wanting a reason for my spellbound gaze. They traveled on the thrust of each other, partners on the journey. Just like us on the farm.

When the lead goose got tired, he took a break and fell to the back of the formation to rest. Another took his place as the formation continued on. Many hands, or wings, make light work.

The geese flew in formation and gave a honk of encouragement to those up ahead to keep up the good progress. Canada geese are among the most talkative animals, with babies communicating to parents even before they hatched. My pond was alive with their chattering! And that encouraged me, as well.

Sometimes a lone goose called through the course of a day, traveling back and forth between ponds along the waterway, looking for his mate who was lost. No goose got left behind: if a goose was sick or wounded, another pair of geese followed it to the ground and stayed to protect it until it could fly again or it died. This was the kind of bird that would stick with you through a midlife crisis.

Why should I care about these silly little short-lived bits of feather? They had flown under my radar for years, while I judged them as unworthy of my animal-loving time. What is the word for "racist" that applies to species of animals?

Bird-watching ended up being a year-round habit, a kind of global positioning method for finding myself, reflected in the feathered creatures who shared my farm. They had lives no more or less important than mine. I had been raised by people who believed in a hierarchy; who thought some lives had more value than others. That lesser lives should be donated to the maintenance of more important lives. Humans seemed like cannibals sometimes.

Yes, I became a bird watcher and found a rhythm in time. A peace in the change of seasons. When winter days were short and dark, I didn't hibernate like a depressed bear. Better to flock together and share the warmth and company of unique individuals, and cheer each other on. I might need to be the lead goose for a bit, but the others will have my back, and I can be lifted by their thrust. I can depend on it.

Equine Professional

Before moving to the farm, I had always loved being an amateur in the horse world. That's the label for someone who doesn't make an income from their sport because it's about more than money. The root word in amateur is the Latin word for "love" or "lover." Being an amateur meant putting love above money, a behavior I had had wild success with. I wanted to be an eternal student, creating a lifelong work of art with my own horses. I couldn't imagine pulling myself away; there was nothing more fascinating to me than *my* horses and *my* riding. I rode at every opportunity. I took a minimum of two or three riding lessons a week. On the weekends, I paid huge amounts to ride for forty-five minutes with famous trainers and Olympic riders. I was a sponge.

My mother asked me repeatedly, in that mom voice, "How long do you think you'll *have* to take lessons?" Like she thought I was such a poor rider that I just fell off the side. My parents didn't want me to get Spirit in the first place and had been mad about it for a few years already. I got defensive at first but I eventually found the answer, "Olympic riders have coaches, Mom. Can you consider it coaching?"

And on I studied, every book I could read, every clinician I could ride with or audit. Being an amateur meant my passion could be so much bigger than a day job. Besides, I loved being a goldsmith. I didn't need a job.

I had the privilege to study with the best. Strangely, lots of trainers don't even like horses. The horse training world is a place where money gets slammed up against the spirit of horses. Owners want results fast and horses are shoehorned into what people wanted them to be. That was frequently a hard squeeze and many young horses became casualties. Nope, I was happy right where I was, totally self-obsessed in my little amateur horse world.

Sometimes friends asked for help with their horses, and I obliged. My horses continued to advance, year after long year of thoughtful training, to more complicated, beautiful work. I was active in the leadership of my dressage chapter; I knew that political side of the horse world. The truth is that all of us in the horse world are very passionate, and swimming around in all that love and emotion about money and horses was dangerous. So I kept my nose where it belonged, right between my own horse's ears.

Right up until I got the job offer I couldn't resist. Just after my fiftieth birthday, I got a call from the barn manager of a breeding farm with a plan to grow. There was one trainer there already, and they were preparing for the arrival of a newly-hired rock star of a trainer from the East Coast. At the same time, the farm had just purchased a bunch of horses, including a new gang of weanlings, less than a year old.

"Do you want to come here and work with the youngest ones? There are eleven foals, between six months and a year old. You'll need to be insured, that means turning pro, of course," the barn manager said. I would be in charge of ground manners, trailer loading, and general introductions to the human world. Six of the babies were untouched, in a big pasture with their feral moms. The other five weanlings had just arrived from a farm half-way across the country, scared and a bit traumatized. I dropped my amateur status like a rock and started within the week.

I arrived early my first day on the job, just as the young travelers finished breakfast and the stable hand was cleaning their pens. I heard him singing in Spanish to the babies, in a low, rhythmic tone. Calm and quiet as he mucked, he gave a scratch sometimes. He respected the babies. Could there be a better job ever?

I met each of the foals one by one, and each weanling was uniquely different. Some wanted to be in my pocket, close enough to step on my foot. One of them was aggressive with a mad-at-the-world bravado. Some were shy and reluctant to be caught. One of the babies was only four months old, much too young to leave her mother and endure the stress of travel cross-country. This little filly was a bit weak and not very interested in eating. I spent extra time with her, sometimes just deep breathing. She needed a boss mare, the kindly sort, to let her know she was alright.

Brash or suspicious are both expressions of insecurity, and confidence is the cure. That's what horses taught me and I passed it on, as I moved slowly and respectfully, and asked for the same response from them. Their good choices were rewarded immediately with praise and soft hands. Corrections were rare, but quick, and neither side held a grudge. I was patient, not pushing for too much too fast and always ending on a positive note. Their partnership with humans was off to a good start.

The boss mare in a herd is the one who moves the other horse's feet, so that was how I started. Once the halter was on, I asked the foal to move his feet, by matching my stride. Slow at first walking around in the pen, and then out to the paths between pens. When there was a scary obstacle, we explored it, sneaking up in slow motion with lots of reward for each small effort. When he eventually touched it with his nose, he got a huge scratch and praise for that. Curiosity is a sign of courage in a foal. Going slowly and staying patiently positive builds a horse's confidence; it trains them to *try*.

The road up to the barn was steep and having four feet doesn't guarantee balance. One reason for so much leading at this point was to teach listening and manners before they top out at a thousand pounds. Negotiating the hill at my speed, one step at a time, was safety for the horse and handler as well. Down the hill a halt was added between each step. There were icy days, and those hills got challenging, but the foals were brave.

Soon we ventured farther on our outings, out of view of the herd. It meant trusting me all the way to the round pen for short release and catch visits. We ventured onto the rubber mats in the barn for grooming, picking up feet, and clipper training. Also getting in and out of a horse trailer, slower than slow, without fighting or pulling. Patience and breath were my training aids.

Everyone worked for the horses at this farm. Two men were caretakers and the original trainer was well-respected. I was there two or three days a week. We were all friendly, and it was a peaceful coexistence. When the new East Coast trainer arrived, days got a lot busier in the barn, but I was out with the feral herd most of the time by then.

There were six mares with foals in a forty-acre pasture. I am not sure how they all got there, but the babies were six months old and hadn't been touched. Ever. They all grazed as a herd and were extremely wary of intruders. In the beginning, I walked out to where they were and hung around for an hour or two. If I got too close they moved off, so when I found that imaginary line, I stood right on it. Sometimes I would turn my back to the herd and take a step or two over the line, and wait, then walk away. I walked to the other side of the pasture and found the line of intrusion there and wandered on either side of it for a while. It didn't take all that long to bore them, and move closer, but just one step at a time, with lots of lateral steps intermingled.

That's right, no rodeo drama. The first week I stood in the field with the herd a couple of hours a day, teetering on the line of intrusion, and then went home. If I wanted to get closer to them, I had to prove I wasn't a danger. Sure, the farm could have roped the mares and dragged the babies along behind. It would have been faster in the short term. But the farm owner wanted to do it right because she knew that in the end, this way was quicker, cheaper, and most of all, less stressful for the young ones.

Eventually I wandered through the herd a few feet from individual mares. My guess was that historically, when these mares were caught, it was for scary or painful reasons. Humans had proved themselves the enemy.

When horses are fearful and distrusting, it's rarely about needles, hoof trims, or getting into horse trailers. What they actually don't like is the fight that happens at the same time. We create so much discord, being in a hurry and bullying them along, that their distrust of us is honest; their resistance is real fear. When human agendas become loud and emotional, we look like dangerous meat-eating predators. Which we actually are, so I respected these horses and their survival instinct.

Now it was time to sell the idea that we might be friends, not with baby talk and treats, but with behavior that is not stalking (sneaking around with a halter behind my back) so much as team building. In this case, after spending hours in the pasture, I was still letting them know that I was not the enemy. That meant I acted like I had all the time in the world. I spent hours *not* catching them.

One of the mares was a bit more accepting than the others, so she was the first I touched. I kept eyes low, moved quietly, just a few inches closer, and then retreated, cocked a hip and after an hour of my mundane, toe-dragging two-step, I lightly touched her shoulder. The second I did, I turned and immediately left the pasture for the day. I wanted them to know that being touched was not the same as being caught. I went home to have a celebratory beer with the goats, feeling so fortunate. People have been meeting horses this way since the beginning of time.

Eventually I did this same touch-and-go game with each mare. Soon I walked among the mares, and paused to offer a scratch as they grazed without creating a disturbance. It took long days, but the mares accepted me. Meanwhile, the foals were still just as skittish as ever. They'd run and buck and stay away. If one or two were quiet enough for me to think about approaching, another colt came galloping through and stole them for a run.

When a foal is born in a pen, breeders use the process of imprinting to desensitize the foals, like I did with Clara. On that first day, the baby got the experience of being handled in a variety of ways, especially wearing a halter. Since horses have such strong memories, they always remember, so it's familiar even after time has passed. Conversely, this mob of foals had a very distinct memory of *never* having a halter or anything else on their face or around their ears. Touching the mares was the easy part.

While in the herd, I tried to see through their eyes as much as I could. Body language was my first and best way of communicating. I was acutely aware of every weight shift, every turn of my shoulder, every breath. There was lots of planning time in this process and I thought of little else. Separating the foals would not get me the result I wanted, so I came up with an idea to use the mares as reverse round pens. When trainers work a horse in a round pen, they get the value of a bend on the circle to relax them, there is no corner to trap, but no escape, just forward on the circle, and the communication is contained.

So now, instead of defining that circle by an exterior fence, I used an interior center point, the mare. I would take a step toward the foal and he would step away from me. Each time the foal stopped, I stopped. We walked circles around the mare. The foal didn't want to leave her, and he felt safe with his mom between us. I maintained my energy level, never quick and no grabbing. I followed his movement to a stop, exhale and again forward, and soon I could influence his feet with mine. The mares were all so used to me now that they didn't miss a bite.

Eventually I got close enough to touch the foal on the rump. Just an instant, then I turned on my heel the opposite way. He turned and followed me. Now he was trying to catch me! Following my feet like he does the mare's. I said a low "Good boy," instead of the fist-pumping happy dance I wanted to do. Some foals felt safer with a touch on the shoulder to start, but soon they would reverse and follow me, and that counted as controlling their feet. I was winning hearts and minds in slow motion.

Does this sound tedious? I loved every minute. I felt so real in the moment, so aware of my body, and aware of movement of the herd on all sides of me. It was primal body communication, like time travel to the wild—to a time when wits mattered more than book learning. My body moved with meaning and honesty. My breath regulated my emotions. It changed me. Even more than my farm, that prairie pasture was my jungle and I was having the time of my life. I knew Jane Goodall would understand.

I worked with one foal for a while, around his dam and then moved to another. Days passed and slowly walls in my herd melted. One foal after another was haltered and led a few steps at a time, away from mom and away from the herd. Icy cold wind changed to showers and grass. All the babies were in halters but one.

And then I got fired. I know, it surprised me too. As far as I knew I was doing a great job. They said the new trainer wanted me out. Maybe it was a power play; it would be hard to imagine I was a threat somehow but he was not a confident man. There's a lot you can tell about a person from the way they work their horses. He worked his hard and without reward.

The barn manager who hired me was fired as well. There was a lot of change in the barn but the East Coast trainer still wasn't happy. A month or two after I left, I heard he got fired. He punched the Spanish lullaby-singing stable hand in the face and the farm owner found her voice.

Politics in the horse world are no different than the corporate world or the art world or any other place. Whether you do a good job or a bad job, life is uncertain. People have hidden agendas. We are always positioning ourselves away from our pasts or toward our desired futures. We are imperfect in a hundred destructive ways. No human communication since was ever as clean and honest as it was out in the pasture.

On one hand, I had traded a monthly insurance payment and my amateur status for a job that didn't last very long, but at the same time, people had been asking me for help with their horses for a while. It meant giving riding lessons and after taking a few thousand of them, I had some ideas about how to help the learning process for humans, as well as their horses. I had a strong foundation of knowledge and awareness, and the creativity required in my first career only blossomed more in the arena, where I saw each horse and each rider was a unique work of art. In my squinty-eyed aversion to becoming a trainer, it hadn't occurred to me that I'd have the possibility of learning so much more than one horse could teach me. Now I had a herd of horses and riders schooling me and a brand new career at fifty. Was I too old for this? In some ways it was daunting but the horses helped me. I'd been borrowing confidence from them since the very beginning—there was nothing new about that.

Part Three:

Stable Relation

Your Soul Mate is an Alien

It was back near the beginning of my beautiful midlife crisis. My feelings were starting to slide around a bit, but nothing too alarming, when I received an unexpected gift. My friend had been to a psychic and I was about to hear every word, "And she knew what I did for work, I didn't tell her. She talked about my mom, you know, so right on..." She was on a rant. This was going to take a while.

I'm not sure what I think about psychics, tarot readers, and the sort. I don't read my horoscope. I believe we make our own luck, even when it isn't particularly great. The future will get here soon enough, I don't want to know ahead of time. On the other hand, I am not a total skeptic. We discover new things that have always been there, like electricity, all the time. We don't know everything—any donkey will tell you that.

Besides, I have tried to encourage my intuition over the years. I notice the more I trust it, the better it gets. I treat my intuition like a cat: I don't try to make it do a sit/stay, I give it a bowl of milk and just watch it out of the corner of my eye. No pressure.

So I didn't ridicule my friend. She felt this reader gave her advice that would help her, and that was good enough for me. Sometimes it's enough to just feel better.

"You will just love her, I got you a visit, too. I already paid for it. Would you go?"

"Why not?" I said. I called the next week for an appointment. Why not?

I remembered a reading from a different psychic years before. She began by telling me that I had a personality that sometimes intimidated men. It made me laugh out loud, "I sure don't need a psychic to tell me that!" She laughed, and I laughed and the tension released. Having a reading was a bit like letting someone search your underwear drawer when you don't know what else might be there.

So I arrived to this gift reading with no agenda. There was a question I had about Spirit that I would ask if there was a chance. Other than that, I was ready to listen. Her office was in her home; there wasn't too much purple or too much poster art or too many candles. I got comfortable enough and she took some deep breaths.

She jumped right in, "You're married but your husband is not your soul mate. He's a bad match for you, not very smart. You won't be together long; you might as well just cut your losses and leave him now."

Well, that was awkward. And blunt. We were struggling, I admit. My husband just got a mental health diagnosis that neither of us wanted him to have, but I was nowhere near quitting. I got a bit defensive but focused on not letting my eye-brows go weird.

She went on, "So much change for you. You'll change careers. Big changes."

Now wait a minute. Even if husbands change, my work doesn't. I've worked hard to be recognized and have shown my art jewelry in galleries across the country. I loved my work, I made a good income. Most people, myself included, thought that the best thing about me was my work. Maybe I became a bit more defensive..

She sounded so excited for me, "You will be working as an intermediary, a facilitator kind of. They will contact you to begin, and then you will connect with humans in their name. You will be interceding between humans and…" She searched for the word, "and… aliens."

Deflated. I had no air in my lungs. Really. Aliens?

The psychic got very excited now, talking about their culture and our culture coming together. "All the people who don't understand are confused and what a help you will be to them. And the aliens, they also appreciate you and praise you to each other."

Oh, great. Aliens will be talking about me behind my back. I kept glancing at the door. How long could this go on? Could she even hear what she was saying? Should I excuse myself and get out now?

Just when the reading couldn't get any worse, she said, "Your soul mate is an alien. You'll meet him while you are working."

I'm pretty sure I got really squinty-eyed about then. First of all, I didn't really believe in soul mates. I didn't think love was that kind of pass/fail experience. I tended to agree with dogs about love; there's lots of it go to around and everyone is worth a wag at the least. Since I'd had a few relationships with different sorts of guys, I didn't know what soul mate meant. Was random dating a waste of time if he wasn't the one? If you're late for the meeting, do the two of you flounder off to other doomed relationships? I might have blown my chance already and I didn't want that to be true. I decided to focus on the soul mate part and ignore the alien part for the time being.

"Your love will be so beautiful that you won't need words and the two of you will work together to bring people together with his…side," she was very excited. She might have even envied me.

Well, she can have him. Will we not need words because he

has no mouth? My mind flips through all of the images of aliens I know from the movies. There was that movie *Starman* with Jeff Bridges but the rest, well, not really my type.

What if she was right? What if my soul mate really *was* an alien? Was there really a need to divorce my husband then? If the alternative was waiting for my alien lover to land on the planet, no, I refused to ask the psychic for a time line. Oy. If I did divorce my husband, was there any reason to date in the meantime? Should I give up dating and marriage and just wait for my alien soul mate?

I listened with one ear while my brain tried to scurry away. Awk. She was cheerful and gave all kinds of details that I didn't want to hear about my career change. Still I was a guest in her home and wanted to be polite. I might have been crazier than she was.

She was finally winding down and I was anxious to get out of there, already planning neutral phrases to write in the thank you card to my friend.

"Do you have any questions I can answer for you?" That hung in the air for a moment. What the hell, I could ask.

"Is my horse okay?" I asked, deliberately vague

She said, "Is he a tall white horse who loves to flash his tail?"

Now she had my attention. "Yes, he is."

She smiles, with her eyes closed. It's like she's watching him and then she says, "He is very lovely. Does he have a friend who is brown?"

Her horse language was not very sophisticated. I responded, "There are bay horses around. Brown horses are called bay."

"Does he have a friend who has a white stripe down the front of his face, and then a kind of black lightning bolt through it?" she asked.

Facial markings are always white. A white blaze with a sideways stripe of black hair through it? That was crazy. I know I had never seen it, ever… until I met Touchdown. He was the stallion who lived in the stall next to Spirit at our old barn. We had just moved to a new barn and Spirit was having a hard time adjusting. Now she had my attention. Riveted is a good word.

Cautiously I answered, "Yes, I know a horse like that."

"Your white horse is worried about that brown horse," she said.

"Bay," I faintly corrected.

She continued, "Has he been hurt? Can you find out how he is and let your horse know?"

"Okay...."

"Any other questions?" she asked.

"No, you've given me a lot to think about." I told the big fat truth that time.

We said our goodbyes and she hugged me as if we had been old friends talking about the weather. I got back to my truck shaking my head. It would be easy to forget the whole thing if she hadn't described Touchdown so well. I called a friend who was still at the old barn.

"Is Touchdown okay?" I asked. He was a magnificent horse, Dodger's sire.

"Touch was injured, you know, and on stall rest the last couple of months. He's doing better now, he'll be okay and all, but there were some scary days. But he's on the mend." She asked, "How did you hear? You been back to the barn?"

"No, a psychic told me. I asked her about Spirit," not a comfortable answer from me. My friend was quiet, not knowing how to respond, and in an effort to lighten the conversation up, I added, "The psychic also said that my soul mate was an alien."

"I haven't had a lot of luck with men on this planet; does your alien soul mate have a friend?" It was just the first in an ocean of bad jokes.

The next morning at the barn, I went into Spirit's run and told him out loud that Touch was okay. That there had been a nasty injury but not to worry, he would heal up just fine. It felt a little awkward delivering the message. Spirit shifted his weight and gave a lick and chew, and then blew loudly, sure signs that he felt better. He asked for a scratch on his withers. He had to take a step forward, positioning his withers right next to me, because I didn't take the cue at first. I groomed him and tacked up. His neck was relaxed and he trotted forward effortlessly. More willing and less fussy. He felt great and I did the thing I always did when life got confusing—I just rode.

But it was hard to clear my head. I wished I had never mentioned Spirit at the reading, she recognized him so quickly. I could have blown off this whole alien malarkey easier without that, but then Spirit was relieved at the news about Touchdown. That didn't help either. Should I be looking for strange lights in the sky now?

In the next month, I told the alien soul mate story a few times and it got a little funnier with each telling. People made hysterical comments. Who hasn't been to a bar where people looked like aliens? We all blew off some steam about bad dates with pseudo-alien lovers and went back to our lives. I brought the story out at parties sometimes, but I didn't think of it again until my divorce. After that, it briefly turned into a reason to not date. I could just stay home until the Mothership landed and my doorbell rang. The story got put away with old tennis rackets and a few pairs of inappropriate women's shoes. No use for them on the farm.

I hadn't thought of the psychic in years.

Once I hit fifty, when I got a call from someone I hadn't heard from in a while, I expected bad news. That same horse friend called to tell me our beloved trainer had passed. I hadn't ridden with her for years, but she was so much a part of my riding mind that I felt like I talked to her daily. She was simply the finest horse person I ever knew.

A few days later her memorial service took place at the meeting hall on the fairgrounds. The mourners included a large number of trainers; it was hard to not do some celebrity gawking. There was a podium in front and just to the left, her beautifully worn hand-made saddle—as familiar to us as her weathered face. On an easel next to the saddle there was a photograph of my wonderful trainer with her favorite stallion, Touchdown. I was choking back tears and gratitude, there was so much respect in the room. Horses everywhere had to feel her loss, too.

As I listened to the mourners reminiscing, my eyes went back to the photo of Touchdown again and again. You can tell so much about someone by riding their horse, and I'd had that privilege. Touchdown had passed a few years earlier. Is there a better epitaph than "She rode good horses"? To think they were both gone from this world led to a hope they were together again now; I prayed that was true. Touchdown held my eye; he was as mesmerizing as ever with that black bolt of color through his blaze and his finely etched muscles. His coat was the color of burnished brass, metallic and warm at the same time. How could anyone call him brown? Such an insult!

I hadn't thought about that psychic and her silly prediction for years. She knew so little about horses that she called this ethereal stallion plain *brown*. It was blindness to see this stallion as ordinary. So ignorant—as little as that psychic knew about horses—they might as well have been aliens.

From Where the Sun Now Stands

My mother was right. I was not a particularly pretty girl. I'm not complaining, I defended myself by hoping life had more to offer than superficial appearances. Some girls struck a high note in high school with lots of friends and a romantic social life. That wasn't true for me, but I had a secret from my youngest years: I believed I would be a cool old woman. I planned for it. There were so many desperately sad adults around when I was growing up, that I started contemplating regret when I was young. Would I regret not having a ten-speed bike? Would I regret not taking French? I noticed no one else in junior high school made decisions this way, but by then it was a hard and fast habit. It stood me in good stead, and today those unhappy relatives get credit for reverse inspiration. I like to think that I've peaked late. But then, I like to think I have a singing voice too.

It is hard to pull out one moment that changed the course of our family. Life inside our house was passively horrific; anxiety was served with the potatoes at dinner. It was our normal. My father eventually learned to harness his anger from violence to slow burning rage. Was it an improvement? Hard to say, the air was always thick with dark emotions. No one laughed. Days were silent. Dad's heavy feet were always audible, stalking from place to place with the weariness of carrying a heavy, long-time grudge. The rest of us walked on eggshells, careful not to disturb the resentful peace.

After losing the farm on Leaf River, my father worked in a plywood plant. He usually worked on a loud machine that punched out knots in the wood and plugged them like a huge paper punch. He hated it. It was dull repetitive work that gave him too much time to think, and all of his thoughts were dark. Truth was, he hated everything. Hearing him watch the TV news said it all: Damn Russians. Damn War. Damn economy. Damn Democrats. Damn Seahawks. Damn rain.

Just before my mother died, she found her voice and began reminiscing. Dad had passed away four years prior and it was finally safe to talk about him. A visiting uncle reminisced that my father was famous for working kids for long hours rather than hiring a hand. He laughed, telling stories about how cheap and tough my father was, my mother chuckling as if it was common knowledge. I had no idea other people knew what went on with us.

"Do you remember the day that he killed that dog? For ripping up those sheep?" My uncle laughed like it was a wildly funny practical joke.

I remembered. I remembered my father's anger. I remembered the dog. I remembered being told it was my fault because I had played with him and that ruined him for herding. There was no talk of dead sheep. My father made me watch him kill the dog to punish me. Now that it was safe, my uncle made the joke and mom laughed along. They didn't notice me then, any more than they did when I was a kid. But I remembered that black and white Border collie. I tried to resist the dog, but I did sneak a scratch or two in. I had carried the blame all that time. It didn't occur to me back then to check the "dead barrel" by the barn for sheep underneath that dog's carcass, but now I wish I had.

This was my mother's second bout with cancer and she finally told me about the first cancer treatment. When we were still on the old farm, she had stayed at the hospital for a couple of months undergoing radiation treatments.

"I worried about you kids being alone with your dad, worried he might kill one of you," she said in a matter of fact tone, as if she was remarking that someone was late for dinner. It was almost the acknowledgment I wanted, now that it was too late to do anything but let go.

Dad came by his temperament honestly; he was raised by a brutal man in a brutal environment and he knew the world was a hard place. He didn't want me to be a victim; he wanted to make me tough. Farms are no respecter of sex or age: work had to be done by those available to do it. Dad taught me to drive a tractor for haying season before I was tall enough to reach the brake. He also taught me to cook. He was a proud and pained combat veteran of WWII who voted for George Wallace for president. A redneck who ridiculed hunters and taught me early to hate guns. Who else could have turned out an eclectic cowgirl like me?

My Leaf River farm legacy was that I needed to be strong and capable and the gender lines were not important. It came as a shock to my father to end up raising a liberal feminist but in hindsight, it was simple logic.

Work as a goldsmith gave me a way to earn a living while being noisy and dirty, both traditional farm skills. I started in the mid-'70s, when it was still considered a man's occupation—a job description we didn't have growing up, so I ignored it. Farming was the original self-employed job and it prepared me for the self-motivated life of an artist.

In the beginning I was gawky and out of step with everyone. I barely spoke out loud but I needed to think I was different, that I could change the past. That I could make myself better. I read literature and learned manners. That combined with a healthy dose of bravado, and I might pass as a slightly more sophisticated girl.

Then one day while I was still in Denver, it happened. I stayed a bit too late at the barn with the horses that morning. I hurried to the gallery for an appointment with a client. Once I got there, I pulled off my dirty muck boots and left them on the front stoop of the gallery. I brushed the barn dirt off and changed into my art clothes. For me that whole "dress for success" advice meant colorful ethnic clothes that washed well. I got my jewelry inventory out of the safe and into the showcases, and the dogs in the back studio room, just as my client arrived. I'd sold her a large diamond already and now she came to see my design for a one-of-a-kind ring to hold it. The total cost was more than my father made in a year.

"There are dirty boots on your front step," my client announced as she came through the door.

"Yes, I just got in from the barn." But my response didn't answer her question.

"What were *you* doing at a barn?" she asked, like it had to be a mistake.

"I have horses, I ride before work." I loved the words in my mouth.

"Oh," she said, "It's hard to imagine you at a barn, I guess."

"I grew up in a barn. Literally." I smiled, revealing my trusty farm girl teeth.

"Really? I always think of you as someone from the east coast, some place like New York or Philadelphia."

I passed! She was dismissive of any activity that might involve dirt, and I'm not saying the woman had much intuition about people, but it happened. With muddy boots and calloused hands, I managed to pass for a city girl. That was the goal since I knew enough to be embarrassed by my rural roots. There's a hierarchy in the rating of the second sex; the city girl classification is a few rungs above farm girl. It was no small transformation and I felt proud that with a bit of effort, I could dress the part. Proud that I had marginally risen above my class, even if I kept my hair short because it was safer with tools and quicker to get clean.

It was all a lie of course, the farm called me every day; some failed farm no one else wanted that I'd rescue someday. When the opportunity came, I jumped fast and landed hard. Then I did a fair amount of howling at the moon just to clear my lungs.

Was it a midlife crisis or did I just need to come home at long last?

I celebrated bad farming and rejoiced spending money in ways we didn't at Leaf River. I had the vet come regularly. There was sweet rest with plenty of green grass for retired horses and llama elders. The financial stupidity of keeping animals who no longer worked was probably enough to make my father hire a horse hit man from beyond the grave, but I could afford to be generous. When the goats got too old to break down fences now, I let them loose. Barn cats with ragged ears and half their teeth slept in the sun on the dining room table. And in this conditional world, it's only dogs who believe in free love. Friendships naturally ebb and flow, the circle of life can't be controlled or altered much, but dog love is eternal. Let there always be dogs.

My midlife crisis had been like a tunnel to daylight. I had come full circle and like the first farm, animals provided me my livelihood again, but this time I worked for them. I trained horses and riders in classical dressage and natural horsemanship. Listening to each half of the horse/rider partnership took my full mind and heart, and twice the creativity and intuition of my previous career. Understanding a horse's physical language was easy but translating that plain honesty to a human was the challenge. We are not a trusting species. I didn't know how long I would be able to continue riding and training, but I became a bit more like a horse every day, and that feels just like being free.

In the end, it's easy to live the dream. You just give everything else up.

Good trainers see a horse's reluctance during training as a fear issue. One school of thought is that a strong leader must dominate horses and push them through their fear. I've had the opportunity to experience a fair amount of domination from that sort of leader and I know it doesn't build trust. Any relationship based in fear is not safe, even if it's as familiar as family.

If we go slow and reward the horse's try, a trusting partner will surface. Horses are honest, they answer in kind to their human. A rider with a different kind of strength can choose to not fight, not create adversity. Instead she could behave like a good lead mare who earns the respect of the herd with quiet confidence and positive reinforcement. When the ride is over, there is a glow of security and deep loyalty in the herd.

It's a gift of humility to have a horse mirror back to you human qualities that you would rather not admit. It might be a passive-aggressive willfulness or an adversarial nature but the big picture is always the same: Once the fight is on, it doesn't matter who started it, because both sides are demeaned by it.

Spirit is an Appaloosa, the horses originally bred by the Nez Perce tribe. If my Grandfather Horse could speak, he would quote their great leader, Chief Joseph who won the respect of his adversaries in war, but in the end, chose peace unrequited. He said, "From where the sun now stands, I will fight no more forever." It's my adopted family's tradition.

The Worst Thing

The worst thing happens on an unremarkable day. It's an experience so bad that it changes your life forever because the part that gets broken can never heal back as good as new. It leaves a scar that sticks out like a crater from a bomb blast and colors everything around it black. It ruins the whole story.

Sometimes the worst thing hits fast and unpredictably, with a searing wasabi-hot pain. Sometimes the worst thing is gradual and deceptively small. It seems like just one more shove, in a long slow pattern of shoves, but this time there's a brittle snap. It isn't loud when the last straw breaks. This pain is cold and dull, and rolls deliberately to the center of your chest to begin turning your heart to stone. After that your life lurches off in a different direction. Sometimes the worst thing takes you so far off course, you become foreign to your own family.

I am done keeping this secret. My worst thing came at me in slow motion. I was twenty-one years old and I still didn't want to get in the car, but my mother wouldn't stop pushing. I'd been living in Colorado for a while and it was my first visit to my parents back in Washington State. Mom asked me to ride with my half-brother back to his house, and then she and dad would pick me up there the next morning. I could tell my half-brother had been drinking. Mom knew too, but it wasn't the first time she had sent me off in a car with a drunk.

My half-brother reminded me of my uncle. Nothing ever went his way but it was never his fault. He acted shocked that the world didn't recognize his special genius. Shocked that grandstands didn't cheer him on, though he never played a sport. But he had one true fan—his mother. When he got a ticket for drunk driving, she blamed the police.

My half brother still had a way of standing too close. He was a bully. He menaced me, like a cat does a mouse.

It was a stand-off. My mother insisted I go with him, and I refused. If I made a bigger deal out of it, we both knew that my half-brother would raise a righteous stink, insulted and angry in her defense. My mother was a small woman; she couldn't make me go along, but I did.

"You haven't seen him in a few years," she practically chirped. "You two need a good visit."

He made a joke about one beer with lunch but it was late afternoon and his breath didn't fool anyone. Mom waved good-bye like we were headed to Disneyland and he opened another beer from the cooler in the car while we were still in the driveway.

We stopped at a roadside tavern after about ten miles and as we sat at the bar, he whispered into my ear, "People think we're dating."

I squirmed away and told him to shut up. An hour passed. I ignored him while he leered at women and told the same stupid dirty jokes my uncle had years before. Every remark was meant to sound like an inside tip, like he was your best friend. I tried to get him to leave, reminding him we had to get to his house where his family waited. When he finished his drink, we drove to the next bar.

My half-brother was an unattractive man, balding with oily skin and a bulbous nose. He thought it was funny to brandish his false teeth, pulling them out to show anyone who would look, while stretching his lips wide with a finger to show his gums—as if being rude was witty. He was different than my father; more like some of the men on my mother's side of the family who sat on the sofa, fondling themselves to affirm their manhood as they demeaned women, judging their cup size.

As if an insult to a beautiful woman on TV was a compliment coming from them. It was excruciating to be around them but at the same time so familiar that it seemed *almost* normal.

Two more bars and two more drinks down the road, and each stop he insinuated himself closer. His breath was in my face as he leered at my T-shirt, all the while flirting with any woman within earshot.

"Hey, Honey, come over here and dance with me," he said, almost yelling, to a dark-haired woman who never looked back at him. Was he trying to impress me? Everyone averted their eyes. I would never tolerate this from a date, but I had no voice, and dread slowed my blood. I kept my eye on his beer glass. We wouldn't leave until he was done.

I didn't know where we were. It was late and he took back roads. We had to be getting close to his home but we stopped at one more bar. This one was particularly dark and shabby with just a few people left drinking. When my half-brother had downed most of his beer, he asked me to dance and then grabbed hard at my hand. What was I doing here? I should have never come. I knew better.

When I cringed and tried to pull away, he changed his mind and put his arm around me, holding me in my chair with a hard grip on my far shoulder. My half-brother leaned in close, just an inch away, then his face twisted and he stammered. I thought he was having trouble breathing, but he was suddenly morose. He told me what sex was like with his wife. He described it in detail with words that were stark and blunt.

"I could show you how I do it," he said. His breath hung thick in the air. No words—I made an ugly face. I just wanted loose.

Then in a little boy's voice, he told me that his wife had had an affair and I thought he might break down. The next minute, he held me harder and turned gruff and filthy.

"I know you screw your boyfriend," he said.

He was like a heavy wet blanket around me; the more I tried to get away, the heavier he became. I was drowning with no idea where we were or how late it was. I was suffocating on shame and needed to get away—to move my legs. I couldn't breathe. Just an inch at a time, I pulled loose and got to my feet and hurried for the exit. He followed me down a short hallway past the bathrooms and he took my arm away before I got to the back door. My half-brother body-slammed me into a corner and pinned my arms tight. I howled like a dog in a trap but no one came. He shoved his hips against me and pushed a hand against my breast. So hard I lost my air. My head knocked the door jamb as his face crashed into mine. I remember the texture of his tongue. My gut turned to cement, and I remember his tongue today, along with the taste of his blood as I bit down.

I didn't feel victory; there was no escape. He was family.

I crossed the parking lot and got to the car, but I didn't know where to sit. The back seat seemed dangerous, but next to him might be worse. I heard hard, uneven footfalls and jumped in the front seat. He was sweating toxic gas. Was his gun in the car? We spun out of the parking lot with screeching tires onto a dark, rain-slick road. I tried to be still but he drove fast and each curve shoved me from one edge of my seat to the other. There was a worn hole in the right thigh of my jeans and I touched my skin there to hold myself together.

It was after one a.m. when we arrived at his home. His wife was up but the kids had gone to bed. She teased us about taking nine hours to drive sixty miles and said that mom had called a few hours before. Her laugh was tight; surely she suspected something. My half-brother and I didn't look at each other. I felt too filthy to sleep but I lay on the bed, fully dressed with my eyes wide open. I heard them have sex in their bedroom down the hall.

The next morning I stayed in their spare room until my parents arrived. My half-brother made jokes with the confidence of a man beyond reproach. He counted on my shame, but he knew even if I had the guts to tattle, nothing would happen. He was protected by women. I didn't want to trust my memory; it would be so much better if it never happened. But it did.

When I got mom alone, I tattled an angry rant through my clenched jaw, telling her what her son did. Fueled by fear and disgust, I raged at her for sending me with him. For all the times she sacrificed me to drunks. She ignored my anger. This time she did not chide me for tattling. Her voice was serious and the answer came slowly.

"You can't tell anyone. This has to be a secret," she said with hard fear in her voice. "You *have to* promise." She said if dad found out, he'd kill my half-brother; she wouldn't be able to stop it. And it would be all my fault. My mother was frail and terrified. She pleaded and I submitted. I went along because I pitied her desperation, even if it was a passive agreement to trade me for him. So the promise to protect my attacker was made, but the dirty secret rotted me from the inside out. Or maybe it was the cool knowledge that if she had loved me, it was limited and conditional. Less than a dog's love.

I didn't come home again for years.

The next time I saw my half-brother was almost twenty years later around the time my father died. I asked him to come outside and I stood tall. I found my voice and confronted him using words I learned in therapy, like sexual abuse and domestic violence. I did what no one else had done; I stood up for me. He was calm and cold as he denied it. He acted like I was a confused child, a hysterical girl. My half-brother shrugged his shoulders.

"I can't admit to something I didn't do," he said, as if it was as obvious as common sense.

A couple weeks after returning home, I received a hand-written letter from him, several pages long. It listed each of his girlfriends and told how each one asked my half-brother to be their first; that virgins begged him for sex because of his gentle kindness. I didn't finish reading it. The words cut my eyes; why did he send pornography? I took deep breaths and thought I would be okay at first, but I started hiccupping, then hyperventilating, then the vomiting began.

Four years later when my mother was near death, my sister and I took turns traveling to her home and caring for her in two-week shifts. Mom was even more diminished and frightened; she had cancerous tumors growing everywhere. One day the hospice worker told us it was time, and one by one she called the men in the family to come and say good-bye. First my sister's husband and then her grandsons. When it was my half-brother's turn, mom was giddy about what to wear, like a suitor was coming. She was coquettish and my heart broke for her. She did not include my sister, my niece, or me in the farewells. We were only women, after all.

By the time my mother passed, her pain had twisted back on itself with suffering enough that her death seemed like a blessing. No one wailed like Clara had when Windy died. My mother's death felt fair; we all had a sense of relief. I never saw her in a moment of joy. I hoped she was free.

Even after my mother passed, I still wanted to doubt the memory sometimes, just for the convenience of it. Just hoping for peace. But the putrid taste in my mouth had never gone away. Our filthy secret affirmed the truth; a forced promise was my proof that she knew it happened just as much as I did. If mom hadn't believed me, her anxiety would have cooled.

My sister didn't pick sides. Other relatives who found out questioned it, but mom never doubted it happened for an instant. Her awkwardness around me in the years that followed the incident was louder than what was unsaid. She had to know her son was a monster. How could she possibly act as if this was normal? Unless for her it *was* normal. Fear had a grip on my mother's heart; she lived in the predator's camp.

With my parents both gone, there was no need to keep the secret any longer. After years of avoiding family gatherings, nieces and nephews finally heard the back story, finally knew I had kept my distance for a reason. There was discomfort on all sides and some denial thrown back at me. It still hurt to not be taken at my word. At the same time, I knew all too well that sometimes it's easier to side with a monster than to admit his existence.

At first, carrying the weight of this poisonous secret did the most damage. It came with a sharp feeling of a door slammed shut behind me. Un-mothered and a conspirator in my own demise, I had no home. The cost of belonging was just too high. It set me at odds with myself and everyone else. Except for a string of therapists twenty years long and a few generations of good dogs.

I didn't fault my mother for not valuing my life. She valued her own even less. And if there was only one chance, only one kind of happy ending for a dysfunctional family—that scene in the movie with everyone toasting each other at the Thanksgiving table, while the music swells and the credits roll—lots of us would be doomed to dismal failure. Healing has more grace than that; amnesty is a peaceful solution. Maybe if the same fight has gone on for decades, it would be a win to just lay it down and walk away.

When I moved to this farm a few months after my mother died, some people told me that it was wrong to put too much value on the furred and feathered lives here. Maybe I do. It isn't the worst thing.

The Best Thing

What little girl doesn't dream of a knight in shining armor on a powerful steed? Even tomboys like me, but it's a fairy tale. Not all knights are honorable. When I seriously needed rescue, I had no trust in humans—I chose a white horse instead. It wasn't that I thought it out. There was no plan. I just followed the well-worn path girls like me have taken for hundreds of years. While some might have sought sanctuary in a church, I found a spiritual safe-haven in the barn. I was made welcome in the herd, like the other lost girls before me. To this day, a deep, slow whisper of a nicker, barely audible, is a balm to my soul.

After the incident with my half-brother, I floundered, continually changing apartments every few months. Relationships didn't last. I spent years re-living that drunken drive, fighting for peace but staying chronically agitated. I tried to prove myself worthy in the world. I gave a fresh, ambitious face to strangers but it was never quite right. Just under the surface, I was unstuck and drifting. Half of the day, I hid my hurt and anger only a bit better than the men in my family. The other half of the day I huddled up like my mother, worried that something else bad was going to happen.

Day by day, my dogs walked me through it. I tried to carve a space between me and the past. I acted strong, I meant to be tough, but it was a lie. I was only protecting my pain. Defensive of my secret. Defensive of my wounds. I clutched my chest tight and trusted no one. And then resented myself for being an outcast.

A sharp weight grew between my shoulder blades; that feeling that the world owed me something. That my pain made me special in a perverse way, and others should show me some kind of preferential treatment. There was something my mother used to say when she talked about someone who had a chronic illness or a terminal fate.

"It's like God put her in this world to teach us all how to suffer," she'd say, with respect, like suffering was a higher calling.

This part felt complicated. The hurt never left me but even if my suffering was justified, did that make it holy? Other people went on living their lives and I was still stuck in a dark bar with a drunk, waiting for someone to save me.

Our memory landscapes are made up of the very best and worst moments standing side by side, jerking our emotions back and forth. It was a precarious existence until I found my balance—reflected in someone else's eyes.

When most people talk about the best day of their lives, it's usually the day they met their spouse or the day their child was born. My shiny-bright best thing in this life couldn't be more obvious: It was that first day in the stall with Spirit. It took me nine years after the assault to get there. I wasn't sure I deserved him even then.

It wasn't easy at first. It took Spirit and me awhile to find our fit. He didn't like people and I wasn't a very stable partner. That first year I rode him, I came off five times. I got frightened and so did he. Every month one of us was injured, yet we were too stubborn to quit and too stubborn to give in. So we picked ourselves up and heeded the first word of our riding instructor, and the most common thing I say in lessons now: "Forward!"

Spirit carried me through love and loss, through life and death. We've been together almost half of my life, but it feels like I was born that day he found me. Eventually he carried me to this farm. It took time but it's true. Any wound can heal. Spirit and I did that just one stride after another. I had a secret weapon: I made my love be one inch bigger than my fear every day.

This is the happy ending: My Grandfather Horse is twenty-eight this year and noble in old age. Would I have ever found my way home without him?

People say he looks good, all things considered. I notice the standard for looking good drops a little more each year, just like his back. But then, the same is probably true for me. The Grandfather Horse rules my farm with a warm eye; we all want to please him. He gets the best stall run at night; a veal pen where he can chew hay and spit it back out, and stay warm. He gets a special breakfast mush, supplements to help him, stirred into alfalfa pellets to settle his acid stomach. He has become a slow, distracted eater and drops most of it on the ground. I give him time.

He was a strong horse in his day. We did it all; we owned our world. He had a gliding canter half-pass, beautiful flying lead changes, and he loved to dance. Sometimes I see a father playing with his child, tossing her in the air and catching her, holding her tight to his chest. Then my heartbeat feels tight in my own chest and I think of Spirit. He did that toss and catch with me.

Now his back is swayed, and the muscles in his thighs are soft and small. He has so much arthritis that from some angles, he has a decidedly bovine appearance. The tendons in his front legs are worn out and he can't straighten his knees. His hooves are flat in front from dragging his toes. My Grandfather Horse leans against the barn wall in the morning and lets the sun warm his bones while he rests his clouded eyes. During the day, he stands just the same way in turnout with his best donkey friend. The only exercise he takes is walking back and forth from his stall with me, slow and steady. He doesn't even feign awkwardness or apology. We're like an old married couple.

Every vet visit adds one more ailment to his chronic list. The most recent one was a moderate heart murmur. I can't panic at this addition. His heart has always taken him farther than his body could go; it must be tired. He has a tumor on his colon, most likely the cause of three years of incurable diarrhea. He has trouble chewing and his eyesight gets him disoriented. Old age is not for the vain, and someday this list will defeat him, but not today. How many horse-crazy little girls have looked into his eye and fallen in love forever? I lost count a decade ago.

Other times he seems to be daydreaming. I slide on the halter, and this horse, who has shadowed my every step for over a quarter of a century, won't move. Maybe he hurts too much or just doesn't want to go. When he was a colt, I put a come-along around his spotted rump to help. Now I wait and cluck, and eventually he shifts his weight. Eventually he moves with me again, his neck long and low as we both take bittersweet baby steps.

Horses have challenged my courage every day and I have done some daring and stupid things in the saddle. Nothing has prepared me for the raw courage and gut strength it takes to watch my soulmate grow old.

The diarrhea is a nuisance. Too much information? Well, we're too old to be embarrassed. We ran out of superficiality years ago. I do what I can to help him, but a change of any sort seems to bring it on, even the weather. His silver hair gets stained with feces and every few days I clean him up. His thick tail takes a bit of work to ease the clumps of manure free, so I get hot water from the house to soak it clean. I sponge off his legs and his hocks. My hands know his body by heart. How many times has my hand touched his shoulder just to feel his warmth? How many times have I bathed him? He has always had an arrogant tail, flashing it with each emotion. He has said more with his tail than most people do with an entire vocabulary. His tail speaks to me still.

My vet says that horses don't get dementia, that instead he is probably losing his eyesight. My vet is wrong. Or maybe there's no difference. Either way he is confused. Either way he has lost confidence. For all of the years that he took care of me, I stand guard for him now. I wish I believed it was as simple as blindness. If I wait out the blank stare that lingers, the random indifference, then I am gifted with an unbearable sweetness as he remembers me. Is this grace?

One day his pain will pass away and he will fly free of his tired body. And my pain of watching his slow-motion decline will pass with him. Neither of us is in a hurry for this time to end. Freedom isn't all it's cracked up to be. Even being bound up together in old age has value.

Every night before bed, I do one last walk-through in the barn. The moon and stars shed all the light we need; there are low nickers and soft eyes as I move through the herd. A simple acknowledgment is all any of us want—just a nod and a touch. When I get to Spirit, sometimes I tell him about my day; that I shared some skill that he taught me. When I do a good job, he gets the credit. I rest my head on his neck and inhale the familiar smell that lets me know I'm home. One more touch, my palm flat and still, tucked in the warm place just under his mane, breathing with my Grandfather Horse. I owe him a debt; he's the one who brought me up in this world.

With appreciation—

To Peter Schuyler for a long run of support that began decades ago in a church gym; for the encouragement to begin this book and then, for reminding me about the elephant in the room but not yet on the page.

To the early readers: Lara Wilbur, Patrick Mcmahan, Sarah Ormond, Pat Miller, Kari Crawford, Lauren Evans, Joy Jahn, and Becky Schooff—who took on the complicated task of reading various drafts and venturing impressions; I'm happy to call each one a friend, good and true.

To my editors, Elisabeth Kauffman, who tweaked, and Diane Alexander, who polished, and then walked with me the rest of the way.

To my Dude Rancher, for being a particular sort of different, and loving the book anyway.

About the Author

Anna Blake was born in Cavalier County, North Dakota, in 1954. She's a writer, blogger, dressage trainer, and horse advocate, residing at Infinity Farm on the flat, windy, treeless prairie of Colorado. Our herd also includes horses, llamas, goats, dogs, cats, and Edgar Rice Burro.

44966493R00135

Made in the USA
San Bernardino, CA
28 January 2017